GONE DOGS

TALES OF DOGS WE'VE LOVED

Edited by Jim Mitchem and Laurie Smithwick

THOMAS WOODLAND PUBLISHING GROUP
CHARLOTTE, NC

GONEDOGS.COM

SAMPSON

FOREWORD

When I was asked to write the foreword for *Gone Dogs*, I immediately recalled all the dogs—and there have been many—that have been part of my life. I can still see them. Every last one. I remember their loving eyes. Their happily wagging tails. Their tongues licking the melancholy from my face. I remember watching them chase balls and catch Frisbees. I remember running with them on the beach, and simply watching them sleep—knowing that they were mine. And knowing that they knew I was theirs.

Like every author in this book, I have said goodbye to too many four-legged friends. But in the end, I think that's okay. Because every moment spent with a dog is precious, and every last one of us can attest to the same truth: To have a dog is to know love.

Lee Clow

Lee Clow is a legend in the world of advertising. Among his many notable works is the majority of Apple's advertising spanning more than thirty years. He also spearheaded the "Dogs Rule" campaign for Pedigree. A dog lover to the core, Mr. Clow continues to be involved with the Best Friends Animal Society and their "Save Them All" campaign, as well as the No Kill Los Angeles (NKLA) shelter.

"Everyone thinks they have the best dog,
and none of them are wrong."

– W.R. Pursche

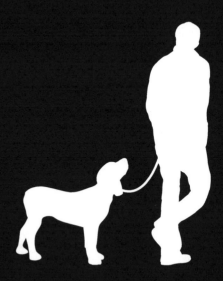

ACCORDING TO SCIENCE, the bond was formed thirty thousand years ago. It was pretty simple—dogs helped humans hunt, and in return, humans shared the bounty. Essentially, we helped each other survive in the world. Today, begging for table scraps is just part of the contract.

As anyone who has ever loved a dog knows, saying goodbye to these partners is hard. Harder than you expect it to be. And for a long time after this impossible farewell, you wonder how you will ever patch the hole in your heart.

But the truth is, you don't. You may be surrounded by dogs all your life, and each one will be uniquely special. And while most of us may never hunt with our dogs, their purpose is as essential now as it was thirty thousand years ago—together, through love, we survive this world. Table scraps and all.

From its inception, Gone Dogs was intended to be a celebration of this bond. A kiss goodnight that will resonate with anyone who has ever loved a dog.

CONTENTS

THE GOOD MOTHER

by Gerry Aldridge

"Here you go, Nina," said Alzira, one of the charming and friendly assistants in the local bakery. She carefully placed a bulky brown bag in the mouth of a small dog that had just followed me in, and the animal promptly turned around and left the shop.

I was intrigued, and so I followed the cute little mongrel out the door and watched her as she ran down the road, took a sharp right up the hill by the bus stop, and then disappeared into the forest, where I presumed she was going to have her own private picnic with whatever goodies she had just been given.

In Malveira da Serra, a magical little village in the mountains of Portugal, anything was possible, so I enjoyed this quaint moment of serendipity, which galvanized even further my love of life in the small mountain range of the westernmost point of Europe.

I asked Alzira about the dog, and it turned out that she had puppies hidden in the woods nearby. Only a week before, she had come into the bakery looking hungry. The women working in the shop felt sorry for her and gave her some food. They, too, watched her run up the hill, but in two minutes she was back asking for more. So they gave her a bag of food the second time, already suspecting she was feeding more than just herself, and in disbelief they watched her run up the same hill, disappear, and then reappear for a third time. They named her Nina.

As the weeks passed, Nina's routine became quite a spectacle, with villagers leaving their houses to come outside and watch. The children would visit Nina and her puppies every day with food, water, and fresh bedding.

The first time I climbed the hill to have a look, I was taken aback. It was October, and the heavy storms were upon us, but someone had taken the time to build a cardboard shelter for the dogs. I did not quite understand at first, but upon closer inspection I discovered that it was layer upon layer of boxes and that there were at least eight puppies snuggled up in different parts of it. Nina sat outside in the rain, keeping watch and getting soaked.

Their plight was precarious, but Nina's dogged instinct to nurture and protect her babies was not going unseen. The whole village felt admiration and astonishment at this mother's determination. It was unanimously acknowledged that this lovely family of animals was not going to suffer, and we would all do our bit to help. I brought them food every evening after work in the storms and gales. Everyone chipped in: this dog family was our collective project.

It was decided that when the time was right, different neighbors would take puppies and give them homes. Before long, the rambunctious little critters found their legs and were often seen playing in the road, cheating death with the cars. Nobody could stand to watch and wait for something awful to happen. It was time.

I arrived at the dog camp on a particularly stormy night to find Nina running around, sniffing and howling and barking insanely. I could not understand what was wrong with her. I knelt in the mud and fed my arms into the soggy cardboard kennel, but I felt no hot tongues or gentle nips on my hands. I delved further, while Nina yelped at my heels, but I found nothing. I then understood that the last puppy had gone, and the mother was now alone.

All her babies that she had so dutifully and lovingly cared for had been stolen. The poor dog was devastated. How intelligent was that dog to have seduced the bakery women into helping her feed and nurture her babies all this time? But this human kindness was impossible for her to understand, and she could not acknowledge the necessity for the tough love we had no choice but to give her.

My wife, Eva, and I already had three dogs, but I had known this day would come and had already realized that we were going to end up with one more addition to our family. Though I had vehemently denied my intentions when quizzed, the truth was that I felt we could give her the loving home she deserved and reward her good-naturedness by taking her out of a hard life on the streets.

I motioned for Nina to follow me home. "Do you want to come and live with us now?" I asked, half expecting her to leap at me with gratitude.

Of course, she was anxious, running around erratically in all directions in search of her lost ones, so I had to construct a makeshift lead to try to get her home. Fully convinced of my cause, I was prepared to drag her if necessary. It was heartbreaking, but I knew that if I left her, she would be lost forever.

Once I led Nina away from the woods and up the street a little, she became a bit calmer, but then she made a sudden dash back to the woods. Luckily, the lead I made with some garden string was holding, and after much coaxing, some pleading, and a little tugging, we made it home. Eva was there waiting with a towel to dry us both off, not quibbling for a second about what I was doing, or why Nina was there. She had obviously known all along that this was going to happen and, as usual, she didn't mind at all.

Our other three dogs—Ludde, the cocker spaniel; Vicky, the Alsatian; and Caya, another mongrel bitch and our dominant female—fortunately welcomed Nina warmly into the pack, and so she settled into family life without any problems. Admittedly, Caya, had to put Nina in her place occasionally, especially when it came to who was going to be the leader of the dog walks, but the hierarchy was soon established, and they all got along very well together.

Nina didn't completely relinquish her freedom, though, and for at least two months we would frequently return home without her after our walks. Let it be said that you can take the dog out of the wild, but you can never take the wild out of the dog. She'd wait until we were far enough away in the mountains, and then she would bolt, ignoring our pleas for her to come back. I panicked the first time, but it didn't take me long to realize that she had gone directly back to the bakery. That is where I would go to find her after almost every time. She always came home with me willingly, though, so I knew she did not want to be completely back on her own again.

Nina ended up dominating the whole household over the course of the years she was with us, and none of us would have had it any other way. This wonderful, doting mother earned a place in our family and in our hearts forever. We learned a lot and became better people because of her. Thank you, Nina.

LAMAR

LAMAR

by Jeff Turrentine

Lamar was a rescue, and so we didn't really know his backstory, but after spending just a few days with him, we invented one that certainly seemed more than plausible, given his many noteworthy idiosyncrasies. He had originally belonged to a hunter, we told ourselves, from the back woods of Chatham County, North Carolina, someone who had (not unreasonably) expected his hunting dog to be able to do all the typical hunting-dog things: heel, fetch, obey the simplest verbal commands, longingly bay when picking up the scent of a varmint, and joyously bark when getting said varmint within its sights. At the very least, we imagined, the hunter had expected his dog to be able to hear a gun go off without cowering in fear and going limp. And so, we further speculated, what a source of frustration this oblivious, untrainable, moodily silent, and easily spooked beagle must have been for the hunter—a frustration that eventually turned to disgust once the three-year-old dog's manifest uselessness as a hunting companion was beyond dispute.

One way or another (accidentally? purposefully but regretfully? purposefully and relievedly?), dog and hunter became separated. When Lee and I first saw Lamar on that day in February of 2002, there at the shelter in Chapel Hill, he distinguished himself by what he didn't do: he didn't, for instance, push his face up against the bars of his little jail cell and make a barking, slobbering, tail-wagging scene as we walked by. He hung back. And not in some coy, playing-hard-to-get kind of way, either, but rather in a way that suggested—heartbreakingly—that he honestly didn't understand where on earth he was, how he had gotten there, or what was going on.

We took him home with us to our rented house in Durham, where we gave him unfettered access—at the (heavily discouraged) scratch of a back door—to a big backyard with plenty of hostas for the digging up, and even a trickling fountain for the cooling of a beagle rump on hot afternoons. On twilight walks we would come across wild rabbits, and some primal impulse would temporarily possess his placid soul: he'd shoot out ahead of me like a rocket, stretching all the slack out of his leash and rendering it straight and taut as a telephone wire.

We made Lamar move across the country. And then we made him move across the country again, and then again, and then again one last time. He never once complained. Home for him wasn't an individual house or an apartment, and it certainly wasn't a particular city or state. Home was defined simply—if repeatedly—as whichever place we all happened to end up together.

He displayed "aggression," if you can call it that, exactly once: on the first night that we brought him home. We had him in a crate in our bedroom. I leaned down to say good night to him before we went to sleep . . . and he growled at me. Sort of. "Stage-growled" is more like it. The effect was largely comical. That was the first time and last time he ever growled at me, or at anyone—or at any living creature, as far as I know. For that matter, he never even barked at anyone, be they friend, stranger, or UPS deliveryman. If you have ever owned a beagle, or have even just spent any time around them, then you know how utterly strange it is to encounter one who is completely silent—as he was. In the twelve years we had him, I'd wager he barked a half dozen times.

He could not be taught to sit, or to stay, or to fetch.

Sometimes he would eat the mail.

He was naturally sweeter—and supernaturally gentler—than any human being I've ever known.

I loved him so, so much.

Bye, Lamar. Thanks, buddy. Good boy.

COCO

"WHO IS LEFT, THAT WRITES THESE DAYS? YOU AND ME, WE'LL BE DIFFERENT."

by Heather Armstrong

What follows was dictated to me on the evening of January 19, 2020. I opened a blank text document on the computer and had no idea what was going to happen. It's long, but it turns out Coco had a lot she wanted to say.

. . . .

Dear Family,

I came to Mom in a dream last night from a spot inside a very peaceful expanse where I have been watching over all of you. **Still watching over you**. My body had to go, yes, but my spirit still has work to do.

I want you all to know that it's okay to cry, but I'd rather hold most of your sorrow about my leaving inside me. Your sorrow is safe here where I am. I have plenty of space to carry it. Instead, I want you to be happy. **Happy and safe**.

Please, all of you, be happy and safe.

Mom rarely remembers her dreams, and when she does they are usually garbled and fuzzy. And I didn't have control of all the details, so I did the best I could. I filled her mind with a room full of women. Everywhere she looked she could see a woman sitting at a desk, and all of them were hammering away at an old typewriter. She could sense that they were working on something important, so she tried yelling, "Why is no one using a computer?!" But sometimes in dreams when you yell or scream the words don't come out of your mouth. So she stood there watching them for what seemed like hours and listened to the sounds of their fingers on those typewriters. Not one of them ever looked up or stopped typing.

It wasn't until the moment before she woke up that she realized I had been sitting at her feet the entire time. And that I had enlisted all of those women to bring this message to her. They were there to tell her that I would be able to talk through her fingers if she allowed me to. She remembered every detail of that dream.

And so, the details.

To E – I call you my teammate because you helped me with my job. I was the quarterback and you were the receiver. And you made sure to get that ball into the end zone safely. You might not know this, but whenever you and Marlo played games together in the basement you were giving me some time off. I didn't know how badly I needed it until I saw the two of you together. I would sometimes check on you, and it was nice to see her feeling so safe with you. Thank you for giving that to me. You are the kindest boy I ever knew (and Marlo thinks the same thing).

To Leta – I started memorizing you years ago. I call you my mentor because you showed me how hard I needed to work to be good at what I do. I never had to take care of you; I only had to *learn* from you. You showed me how to be patient. You showed me the beauty in the repetition of things, because in that repetition we always got better. Those early mornings with you, alone together, were the best moments we ever shared. The silence was so peaceful, and I studied. I memorized your schedule.

Remembering your minute-to-minute schedule helped me savor the time I had during that silence with you. I knew the exact moment you'd come down the stairs, the exact moment you'd leave to catch the bus. More than that, though? I remember what it was like to feel the rhythm of your body when you played piano at night. It's one of the things I miss most. Like you, I memorized all your concerto and solo pieces. I daydream about all of those notes out here as I wait.

To Pete – my father, who never spoke a cross word to me. You wouldn't ever let me on the bed. But in the grand scheme of what you gave to me, I must say . . . what a privilege it was to be welcomed into your room and sit at the foot of the bed on the side where your body lay. And even though I know you didn't do this just for me, I sometimes pretended that you installed whatever it was that made Mom's phone go BOOP BE BOOP when the garage door opened because you wanted *me* to hear it. That noise on Mom's phone meant you had just come home. Was there a more glorious moment in the day? No. There never was. That noise on Mom's phone was better than bacon falling out of the sky.

You loved me, and I felt it and I knew it. And even though I was supposed to protect you, you are the one who made me feel safe. You cradled me with your love. I felt young and fierce and capable of anything. I remember once looking up at you as you stood on the deck outside the family room. I darted around trying to catch your eye, then barked and hunched down as if asking you to play. But I didn't want to play, I just needed some way of getting you to smile and say my name the way you did. It's the same voice Santa uses when he says, "Ho, ho, ho!" In a deep, bellowing, baritone voice. I remember the light on your face. I remember the blue shirt you were wearing. I remember you had on the green shoes. When you smiled and said my name I always found peace, and when my spirit is ready for that glorious beam of light, I have no doubt that a voice that sounds exactly like yours will be calling me through it. And I will run straight at it.

To my lovely R – the promotion I always wanted. You see, Marlo was my first job, and I worked hard to prove just how good I was at making sure she didn't fall off a cliff or go running naked into the woods. I did such a good job for years and years and years that I always believed my mom would give me someone else to take care of, someone else to protect. I could feel it, and something told me it would happen.

And then came you.

Except, you didn't need much protection. You were always so strong and determined. And it didn't even take more than a day to realize that getting to live with you was *the reward*. It was the best reward anyone ever received for working as hard as I did: **I got you.**

I loved your smell and your tiny arms and legs, the way they fit around my torso. I loved the way you hugged my head every morning and laughed every single time I rubbed my back on the carpet and made stupid, dumb noises as you ate cereal. I did that *for you*. Because I thought it would make you happy. I was always excited when Pete would come home, but when it was both of you? OH! I was so excited.

This next part is so important for you to know, R. That last day of my life when you walked in the door I heard you wailing. I heard you scream something about losing a member of your family because I had to go. And it hurt me so deeply to know that you were feeling this because I knew that pain. I had lost so many people in my life. I'd wake up one day and they'd be gone, and I didn't ever get to say goodbye to any of them. I didn't know how I was supposed to feel about it because **I had a job to do**. A dog with a job can't mourn. But then your sadness told me that it was okay to feel sad about losing someone. And I was. **I was so sad**.

Before the vet showed up that day, you were holding me and I was resting my head on your shoulder, and I was mourning all those people I had lost because you gave me permission to. You held me and made me feel safe enough to rest my head in that sadness. You gave that to me before I died. You let me cry with you.

I got to release all of that pain before I came here, and I will tell you how important that was.

But first, I have to talk to Marlo.

Marlo was my life's work. She, my most precious and unique and wild companion to my soul.

Yes, that's what you were to me, Marlo – my soulmate. You were a mirror into me and I was a mirror into you.

No one had to tell me when they brought you home from the hospital that you were my calling in life. I knew immediately and I went straight to work. I never left your side. At least, I never wanted to. Sometimes I got forced into my kennel when all I wanted to do was watch you sleep, when all I wanted to do was stare at your chest and study the way the breath would fill your tiny body. I loved you the moment I saw you and you were mine. ***Mine only***.

I was born into this world to protect and to love Marlo Iris Armstrong.

Every memory I have of my life has you and your dimple lingering just to the side of it. Because you never left my mind, Marlo. Not once. We forged a bond so tight and unbreakable that even when my hips and my legs couldn't take it anymore, I still wanted to walk with you to school. I still wanted to be seen with you and your rainbow socks and say hello to all your friends and make the best impression I could.

You, Marlo, are the culmination of my life's work. You are what I built from the ground up. You are what and who I will be remembered for. And I am so proud.

You, my beautiful blooming Iris, are my legacy.

Every day of my life I held onto the touch of your hand, to every embrace, every kiss, every scratch you gave me. I collected all of them. And ***that*** is what I used to have the strength to let go. My body was going to take me whether I wanted it to or not, and in order to go with my mind and my knowledge of all you still whole and complete, I had to find the will to let my body take me.

It was important that I go with this library of who and what and when and where *intact*. It's why I am still here watching over you. It's why I haven't yet been called by that smiling, celestial voice into *where*? **I don't know where**. I don't need to know. I trust it because it is letting me wait until you have decided to bring another body and soul into our home.

That new soul will need to know some things that only I will be able to communicate to it. This is what dogs can do. I am waiting here so that I can whisper into its ear certain special things, things only I know. Years from now you're going to shake your head and think, "Coco told you that, didn't she?"

Yes. It will have been me.

I love you, **Mom**. Yes, I was the best business partner you ever had. We kept that ship afloat, didn't we? And I knew before you told me that **you've got this**. I just needed you to realize it for yourself. I needed you to feel it. And when I saw the realization in your eyes, I held onto the memory of Marlo's embrace . . . and let go.

Love, Coco

OLIVER

OLIVER

by Cress Barnes

Oliver. The first "child" of a dating couple. Except, no pets were allowed in our small 1920s upstairs apartment.

"Whatever," we said when we saw the black Lab–pit mix puppy crawling out, filthy, from under an old porch at a mechanic shop. "Oh yes! We will take him home!"

We both worked at a nightclub, and during the day Oliver came to work with us, loving the chase game my boyfriend played with him on the empty dance floor.

We didn't have a fenced yard, and Oliver routinely used a busted windowpane in the downstairs French door as an exit to roam the neighborhood filled with elderly people, rentals, and halfway houses. When he dug up our neighbors' flowers, we hid him from the landlord.

One time he brought home a Thanksgiving turkey carcass someone had handed him. Whenever he returned from our downstairs neighbor's apartment, he smelled like weed. (And looked quite happy.) Oliver was everyone's dog.

We grew up. He grew up. We got married, bought a house, and had kids. Oliver's muzzle grayed and he began to move slower, but he watched over his two human brothers like an old warrior. When our third son was born, I knew our time with Oliver was coming to a close. After he died, we spread his ashes where that old apartment once stood.

He was the best dog. Oh, and that third kid? We named him Henry Oliver.

DOBI

ODE TO DOBI

by Holly Kramer

I have many memories with Dobi. Some fun, some adventurous, and some frustrating. She's been a destroyer of beloved items, a backpacker, a coyote howler, a leg-humper, a washer of heads, a master of over thirty tricks, a model for Petco, a website owner, and a superstar. She's traveled far and been on helicopters, trains, planes, cars, trucks, kayaks, boats, and bikes.

As a pup, she once bit a bee and was stung on the tongue. I thought, "Well, this is the end. It's been a good run, my friend. I love you forever." With the help of tweezers, she made it through.

Later she chased a snake with her buddy Homer. I thought, "Well, this is the end. It's been a good run, my friend. I love you forever." They both made it through.

At Zion National Park, she chased a deer, only the deer turned to face her. I thought, "Well, this is the end. It's been a good run, my friend. I love you forever." She ran fast and made it through.

When I lost her in the hills of San Diego at two a.m. chasing a pack of bunnies and then heard the coyotes howl, I thought, "Well, this is the end. It's been a good run my friend. I love you forever." Though my heart was weakened, she made it through.

The time she romped on the greenbelt with another dog, playing and rolling around enjoying the chase and being chased—but when I saw it was a coyote and several others were waiting at the edge of the grass, I thought, "Well, this is the end. It's been a good run, my friend. I love you forever." But she escaped harm and made it through.

When I came out on the patio to find her mouth coated in blue rat poison I thought, "Well, this is the end. It's been a good run, my friend. I love you forever." After an ER visit, activated charcoal, and loads of vitamin K, she made it through.

When she fell out of a car going 60 mph, I thought, "Well, this is the end. It's been a good run, my friend. I love you forever." Stitches and a cast, but she made it through.

Then at eight years old, she got glaucoma and I thought, "Well, this is the end. It's been a good run, my friend. I love you forever." With surgery she made it through . . . barely.

After glaucoma surgery she went into acute kidney failure and came close to her last breath. I thought, "Well, this is the end. It's been a good run, my friend. I love you forever." Thanks to a rotisserie chicken, she made it through.

When I put her on a plane to Hawaii at twelve years old and she came out dehydrated with a bloody, swollen paw, I thought, "Well, this is the end. It's been a good run, my friend. I love you forever." But she made it through.

When an island critter bit her and her face swelled up like a balloon, I thought, "Well, this is the end. It's been a good run, my friend. I love you forever." She made it through.

And now, at sixteen, she is tired. Her limbs no longer move in the direction she asks them to. Many times I have thought, "This dog will not die!" But she will, and when she does, I will say "Well, this is the end. It's been a good run, my friend. I'll love you forever." I hope I make it through.

BEAU

DEAD DOG

by Lisa Underwood

He was not old.
It was not
his time.

I will spare you
the drama
except to say

I lived
in the pupil
of his eye.

RICK

RICK

by Erin Birdsong

Ricky was my first soulmutt.

I was eleven when I got to pick him out of his litter. A large group of little terrier mixes born on June 15, 1995, all black and tan except one. My Rick. He was brown with a black stripe down his back. He was different, an outsider in the crowd. Just like me. I was going through a rough time, diagnosed with depression not even a year before. My medicine wasn't quite figured out yet, the bullies at my new school were relentless, and my maternal grandfather had just passed from cancer.

My parents didn't want a dog. They were very much cat people, but I came into this world knowing that there was a dog out there for me, and I was never shy about asking for one.

I studied dogs. I knew all the big breeds, all the small breeds, and all the breeds in between. I asked for a dog at Christmas, on my birthday, on Wednesday, even from the tooth fairy.

But I think it was the depression that convinced my mother a dog was right for me. Her thinking was that a dog would draw me out of it. He would be my companion, my only friend. Something I desperately needed at that point in my life.

Rick not only became my companion, but my family's faithful companion as well. Every member of my clan had their own special relationship with him, from my newborn cousin to my aging grandmother. We all loved him dearly. And in turn, he loved each and every one of us. He was protective to a fault, nearly biting the UPS man on more than one occasion. He loved wintergreen mints, preferring to take the wrapper off himself. He ran the hill between my house and my grandmother's house multiple times a day, determined to check on everyone. He squealed with joy when he saw someone he loved, lifting his top lip in something that resembled a snarl but was really his own version of a smile. He ran alongside my dad on his golf cart all the way down to the creek behind our house. He killed more snakes than we could count (both poisonous and the good kind) and was never once bitten. He ate the ham-and-mayonnaise sandwiches my grandmother fed him daily. He wouldn't eat it without the mayo, she'd say. Yes, Rick was exactly what we all needed.

And one night, he became what someone else needed too.

It was late, dark, and very cold. Ricky tended to bark often, sometimes at obvious threats and sometimes seemingly at the wind. But this night in particular, he was incessant. He barked for hours on end. We couldn't figure out why. Nothing was out of place; nothing caught our eye. It sounded as though he'd get farther away for a while, but he'd always come back to the door and bark. I thought maybe I heard something at the door, but by the time we got there, nothing was suspect.

The next morning, my mom and I had to go out of town to get my passport sorted. I was visiting overseas for the first time, and it just so happened that our town's passport camera was on the fritz. So we traveled about thirty minutes away to stand in line, and that's when my mom's phone started to buzz. It was my dad on the other end.

Once my dad had gotten up and moving that morning, Ricky had made it clear that he was on a mission. He'd bark at my dad, run halfway to the creek, then run back in apparent frustration. My dad eventually gathered that he was to follow, so he got on the golf cart and gave chase.

And at the water's edge, where Rick brought him, there was an elderly woman in nothing but her dressing gown and socks. She was ill with Alzheimer's disease, had somehow left the warmth of her home during the night, and in her confusion wound up far away. She had survived because of Rick. He had tried telling us the night before, just as he had tried telling my dad earlier that morning. He knew that this person needed help, and he didn't give up until he brought help to her.

The police were called, and her family was notified. When the local paper ran the story, they claimed a search party had found her. There was not one mention of our beloved Rick. He didn't get any outside recognition, no award, no medal or badge. He got a hamburger or two from the local drive-in joint up the street and a few extra pets and mints that day. And every day after.

Rick lived to be thirteen. And on October 17, 2008, we all reluctantly said our goodbyes.

He had a good life. Not the life of a celebrated hero, but the life he loved. Besides, he was my family's hero. And mine, too, in many ways.

THE WONDER OF DOGS

by Angela Wix

Dogs are mysterious creatures. They show us how to keep things simple while reminding us to wake up to the grandness of life. To revel in the taste of a treat. To be consumed by the thrill of the chase. To lounge in the warm sun. It's a perspective we often sorely need and a legacy that is genius. How else can you explain why we bring them into our lives knowing fully that we will suffer their loss? Dogs fill a void—they connect us to nature, remind us how to play, and feed our spirit.

When we truly let them into our heart, dogs act as mirrors that help us understand ourselves better. Physically, mentally, emotionally, and spiritually, dogs reflect our own reality. And while this reflection reveals our strengths, it also shows us where we have room to grow. This quickly becomes apparent when training a new dog. Your frustration becomes their frustration. Your impatience becomes their lack of focus.

Yet when you allow a dog to guide you into places only they can, you begin to experience a world beyond normal boundaries. Dogs open us to mystical wonder.

All this was true of our dog, Jasper. Our first night with him established the foundation for the rest of our time together. My husband Luke, Jasper, and I went out to the drive-in as a "new-family-bonding date." During the show, Jasper crawled onto my stomach and fell asleep. As the night went on, he gradually nudged his way higher and higher until he was shoved up against my chin. I hugged him tight, and my puppy-momma heart broke open. There was no turning back.

I often called Jasper my biological dog-son because we were bound in unexpected ways. We had medical challenges so similar that by figuring out his issues, I was better able to understand some of mine. When I look back at the first picture we ever saw of him, it is obvious he was sick from the start, though we hadn't recognized it at first. Our first year with him was a steady stream of vet visits, new medications, changing dog foods, and repeated medical treatments. As first-time puppy parents, we were overwhelmed, but eventually we found our way. We ended up moving Jasper to whole foods and natural toys, which motivated me to take similar steps in my own well-being.

Living with another being who shared my challenges and quirky characteristics was helpful, validating, and reassuring. Together, we could create our own version of normal. It might have been a hassle to pack a cooler with all of our food for just a single-day outing, but it was also comical. "Who else does this?" I would say to Luke as we stacked containers of meat with bags of fruits and veggies.

Jasper was an empath who felt things deeply. Our vet, who was wonderful at helping us manage his delicate nature, humorously described him as "emotionally fragile"—a description I could personally identify with, and that was spot on.

The comfort we brought Jasper was something he returned to us. He reminded us to love, speak gently, and be kind. He would boop my nose with his to wake me in the morning, a kind of soft "hello." And on his cuddle-bug days, he would ask us for hugs and kisses over and over again, showing how to do it properly: head to heart, fully in the moment, and all weight into it. If Luke and I gave each other a hug, he was right there, shoving his way in to join us. He was most content when we were all together—the happy third wheel that made us feel like an official family.

Sometimes Jasper seemed to understand life better than the rest of us. When my sister-in-law walked into the house one day, Jasper bounded down the stairs to meet her and immediately bopped her in the stomach with his nose. A startled look crossed her face as Jasper obsessively worked to get at her belly. While he was an excitable greeter, this was a bit unusual.

"Jasper, no!" I scolded.

"It's okay," Kim said, guiding him away from her with a smile. But Jasper continued to be magnetized to her. She eventually revealed that she was pregnant. Jasper knew. When our niece was finally born, Jasper's interest shifted from Kim's belly to the baby girl. He loved her face. He loved her diapers. He loved her running, squealing, and giggling. He appreciated her dropped food and, as she got older, he enjoyed her adoring hugs. Their relationship was something special from the first moment.

Five months before Jasper died, a psychic told me she'd seen an image of Luke handing me a kitten. I immediately tried to push it away. "There's no way that would happen," I told her.

"Really?" she asked. "The image is very persistent. He keeps handing it to you, again and again." I shook my head, seeing the image in my own mind: a fluffy little fur ball cradled in Luke's cupped hands, brand-new and full of joy.

"No," I said more firmly. Our old cat had spent half her life resisting Jasper's manic obsession with her. After she passed, we knew we would never get another cat until after Jasper was gone; he loved them just a little too much. So if this woman saw a cat in my near future . . . I didn't want to even think about it. I couldn't imagine losing Jasper.

With this seed planted, my sense of gratitude heightened at the same pace as my worries. I tried to live in the moment, as Jasper had taught me. I focused on the angora softness of his bright-white fur. I savored his mooing groans of irritation when we moved in bed at night, disturbing his slumber. I kissed him uncountable times and held him tight, feeling his warmth in my arms.

Still, I couldn't banish my fear. I hoped I wouldn't have to let him go so soon—after all, he was only eight—but as the days wore on, signs of illness crept in. Mantras of, "Good boy, you're a good boy . . . such a good, good boy," whispered in his ear changed to, "If you need to go, you can go. Thank you for letting me be your momma. Thank you, thank you, thank you . . ."

The last weekend we had together—still blissfully unaware that cancer was taking him away from us—was the first beautiful weather we'd had that April. The grass was green, the sun was shining, and we could finally start to feel the promise of warmth. I sat weeding a flower bed while Luke put together a new wheelbarrow next to me. Jasper lay nearby—lazily sunning and soaking in the simple joy of us being together.

Less than a week later, Jasper died during exploratory surgery. I will never forget the slow-motion snapshot moments of that morning: Luke and me kissing and hugging him in a family sandwich, the feel of his paw in my hand; him trotting away off the front porch and down the walkway into the morning sun. And then the call from Luke hours later. I knew what he'd say before he said it.

Signs of Jasper remained after his passing. The day after he died, I was somehow able to get deep into my work. I was locked in, listening to music and typing up notes. There was no room for my mind to wander, but suddenly I heard, "Oh, so that's what you do all day!"

Startled, I focused in on the source of the voice and saw Jasper in my mind's eye, smiling and wagging his tail. The feeling of his connection was comforting, and I hoped he would come to me again.

A week later I dreamed that I was at an unfamiliar house, touring the space as though it was for sale, yet I felt that it was mine. In the next instant I was hugging and petting Jasper. I didn't share the dream with anyone, but later Kim revealed that she had had a dream visitation from Jasper as well.

"I walked into a house that wasn't yours, and Jasper came running to greet me as usual. He jumped up and hugged me around the neck and gave me a quick lick on my chin. Then he got down and started frantically licking my stomach. I was happy to see his face and give him a smooch. He was such a good pup."

I couldn't believe the similarity of our dreams.

"I think he wants us to see that he's happy in his new home," I told her.

I've always said there's a reason that when I go to type the word "god" my fingers often type out "dog" instead. Our canine companions are some kind of divine guidance. They teach us how to be authentic. They embody a purity that shows us how to be better. When we fall in love with them, they become a mirror so that we may better love ourselves.

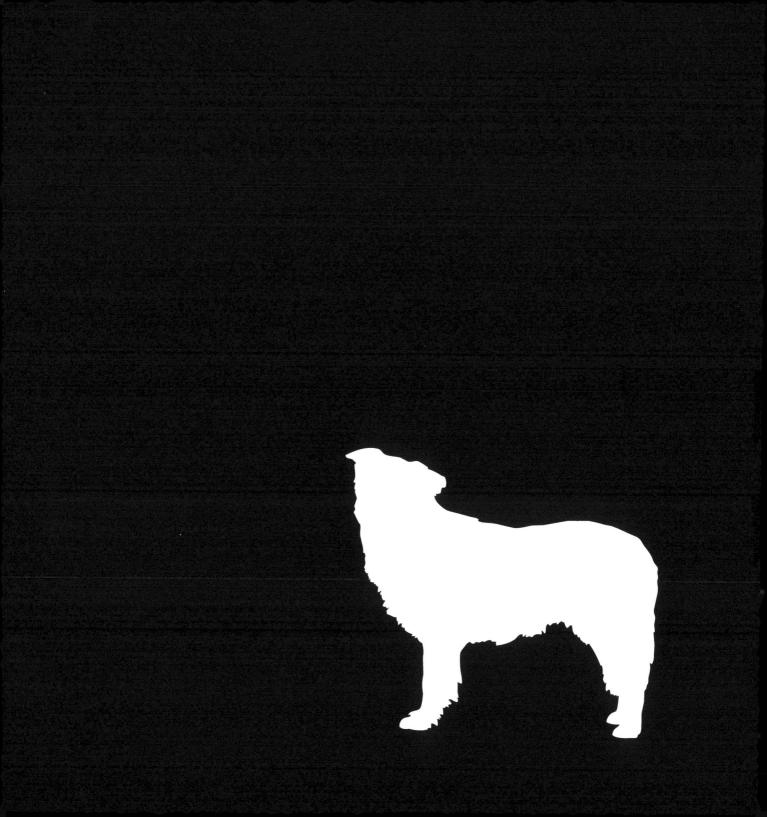

CHARLIE

CRAZY KID

by Mark Gaw

How I wish for you today

You snuggling me in a chair

You touching my leg with your wet nose so that I pick you up

You wanting to be with me wherever I go

You making me smile and laugh

You sleeping in my lap

You being my sweet little boy

You being the best dog in my life

How I wish for you today

GONZO

WHAT WE OWE

by Holly Sinclair

My dog, Gonzo, is a true mutt. A Heinz 57. He's a stocky desert scavenger with thick, red-brown fur, white paws, ears that flop over, and a tail that curls up. The day I rescued him from a parking lot adoption event in Arizona, he was a scrappy looking thing, just three months old, panting in the sun. It was 2001 or 2002, I'm not sure. I do remember that he rested his chin on my knee the whole way home. I had adopted him with my then-husband, but when we split up there was no question about who would get the dog. Gonzo was mine.

My post-divorce period was rough, but I was glad I had a faithful friend by my side. When I threw a glass down on the floor just to hear it smash, then slid down along the kitchen cabinets, plopped my butt on the cold tile and began to cry, Gonzo pushed himself onto my lap and licked my face. We lived for a while near a rocky preserve in Phoenix, and every day we'd hike it, sometimes stopping warily when a coyote trotted past. The only place I could afford to live at the time was considered a semi-tough neighborhood, but I never feared because Gonzo's heavy growl and sharp, sudden bark hid his gentle, mama's-boy nature.

Time passed, and the heartache passed with it. When I'd put on a record and sing along, Gonzo would leap with me as I danced, thinking it was a new form of play. At night, he'd settle down on my feet or stretch out along the length of one of my legs, leaning his entire body against me. We vacationed together, driving from Phoenix to Mexico, and from Austin to St. Louis, and all the way back again. On the Mexican beach, Gonzo's herding nature took over. He'd nip at my ankles when I went toward the water. When I dove into the waves, he'd whimper at the shoreline. Then, desperate to be with me, he'd paddle after me and nudge me with his snout back to shore. My favorite picture of us is on one of those beaches: I'm leaning down to scratch his head, and he's smiling up at me with a doggy tongue hanging out to one side. Over a decade together, Gonzo became my little furry son. We were like Velcro.

After moving back to the Midwest, settling down, and dating again, I met Chad, another dog-lover. We felt comfortable together. We wanted the same things. As we gradually fell in love, we began talking about moving in together. There was just one problem: he had a rescue dog too. A big, lovable problem child named Braunschweiger.

Brauni was a brindle-black Rottweiler mix. An irrepressible, slobbery, ninety-pound love beast. The kind of pup who'll throw both paws over your shoulders when you walk in the door, and then run for a stick or a rope or anything for play.

When I first met this pair of gruff loners, I couldn't approach Chad when Brauni was in the room. The minute I tried to hug or kiss my boyfriend in front of him, Brauni would leap between us and bark. It took quite a while for him to get comfortable with me sitting on the couch next to his human.

The whole experience reminded me of the time, after months and months of sleeping alone, I'd brought a man back to my place. Gonzo had tolerated this other creature in my bed, but chewed up one of my most expensive bras to express his disapproval.

Clearly, I'd been through this before. I figured I'd have to give Brauni time to warm up to the idea of another person in the house. Not to mention another dog.

Unfortunately, unlike Gonzo, Brauni hadn't been socialized or trained as a puppy. Chad had been away at work too often to fully fix the problem when Brauni was young. Then I came into the picture, and now here we were: two loners with two protective dogs. What were we to do?

We took it slow. After consulting a dog trainer, we began walking the dogs side by side, several times a week. Brauni would leer at Gonzo with the unsettling expression of a playground bully.

"Does that look mean he wants to play with Gonzo or kill him?" I asked.

The dog trainer introduced us to a halter-like device for the more-aggressive Brauni and gave us instructions that sounded hopeful. We figured the dogs would either fight it out once and then become fast friends, or simply tolerate each other in their golden years.

As weeks of this uncertainty dragged on and we doggedly walked our two old mutts, I started to move in. Sort of. It started off small. I brought over some books, pictures, a comforter, and a few towels. But we both grew impatient. I was tired of driving a half hour whenever I wanted to visit my boyfriend. It felt silly to leave his house at night when his home felt so much like mine—with my art on his walls, a few pieces we'd both picked out waiting to be hung up behind the sofa, and a new shelf for our shared bedroom.

We helped each other mow the lawn. We wandered through Ikea, bickering mildly and then holding hands like a comfortable, middle-aged married couple. And so it was that we became each other's family.

But our pets were family, too. And whenever I thought of my fifteen-year-old best friend, I worried for his well-being. We could not reconcile our happiness with the incompatibility of these two furry stepbrothers. After all, what do we owe our animals? How can we say which relationships, animal or human, are more valuable? More necessary?

The day we decided to get the dogs together—that is, let them loose in Chad's fenced backyard and hope for the best—we were prepared. We called the dog trainer, a friendly man with years of experience. We wore Brauni out, walking him around the block several times and pacifying him with treats. Then we walked him again, side by side with Gonz, like we'd done for weeks. Finally, we nervously led the leashed pups through the gate.

The trainer watched as Brauni strained on his leash, panting, his eyes fixed on Gonzo, his legs taut. As Gonzo sidled away from Brauni again and again—glancing at me, ducking his head—the trainer frowned. Finally, the man shook his head.

"You guys. This just won't work. I'm sorry."

He explained to us that Gonzo was too old and too feeble—and Brauni was too aggressive—for them to "fight it out" and eventually get used to each other.

"It would be like a really muscular forty-five-year-old beating up on a hundred-year-old man," he said. "I just can't in good conscience recommend it."

Chad mumbled a few sentences about the possibility of someone else in our families caring for Gonzo, and I looked down at my old friend who was, at that moment, biting at some grass and trembling a little. I interrupted the men.

"Well, I'm gonna take Gonzo home. Chad, I'll call you." Then I led my dog away, closing the gate behind us. As I guided Gonzo to the car and watched his legs quiver a bit before he hopped in, there were tears in my eyes because I knew what I'd have to do.

Gonzo and I sleep late on Sundays. With my little full-size bed pressed against a big window in a turn-of-the-century flat, we open the curtains and look down on our neighbors. Gonzo growls low at the cats and wags his tail when I say, "What a good guard dog."

I get tired of living here sometimes, in a rented apartment, while my sweetheart lives in a house so far away. My lonely place, with its bare walls, resembles a student's garrett, but my loyal doggy friend is happy. So I try not to feel impatient or resentful, even when I'm driving across town to visit Chad.

I took Gonzo to the vet recently, and she told me that he has arthritis in his spine. There will come a day, probably in the next year, when his back legs will simply give out. Already, one leg spasms at times, which startles Gonzo more than anything else. I give him anti-inflammatory treats, special food for his joints, and lots of meat—because he loves meat. And I love him.

Sometimes, I swear, Gonzo knows. He looks steadily at me, and then licks my face when I start to cry.

There's no question. I'll be his friend until he's gone. And then, after, I'll have time to make a home with the human I also love.

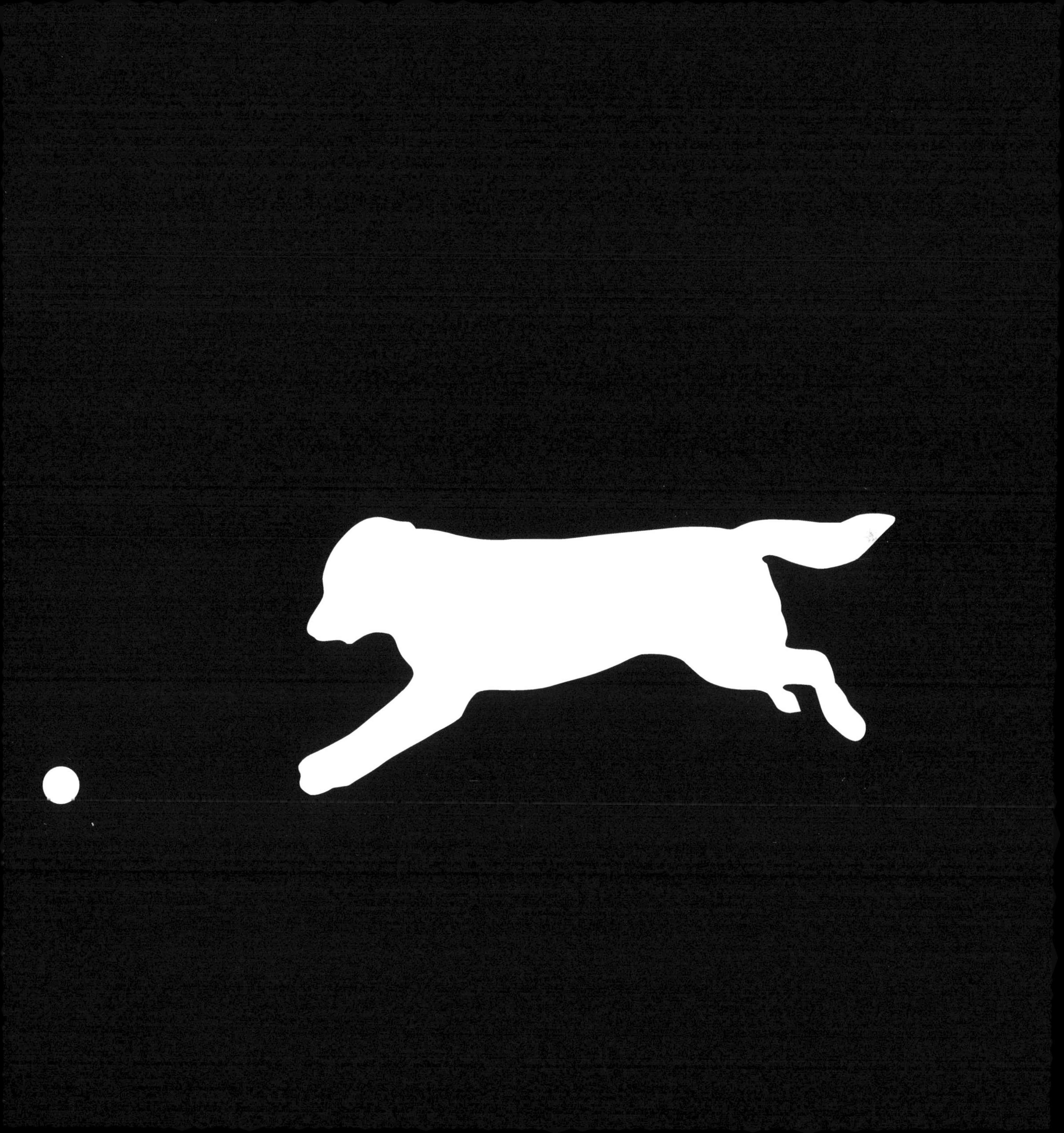

DUDLEY

DUDLEY

by Judy Goldman

We all loved Dudley beyond words. He was the cutest dog any of us had ever seen. He was a black-and-white cockapoo, curly and cuddly. All you had to do was say his name, and he wagged his tail so hard it became a blur. The expression on his sweet face said, *I may not be perfect, but my love for you is.*

And perfect he was not. Why not?

If he got one of your socks, you just had to let him have it. When out-of-town company came, we gave two bits of instruction:

1. Keep your socks off the floor.
2. If your sock ends up on the floor and Dudley gets it, just consider it his.

One guest did not listen. He left his sock on the floor, Dudley found it, our guest tried to pull it out of Dudley's mouth, and the guest came running downstairs, yelling, "Your f   ing dog just about took off my arm!"

Dudley considered the mail dropping through the slot in our front door a personal affront. The minute he heard the clink of the brass and the thud of mail hitting the floor, no matter where he was in the house, he ran as fast as his legs would carry him, growled and clawed the offending door, and ripped the mail to shreds—leaving the scraps on the floor of the entrance hall like confetti after a parade. Ask my daughter why she had to write to Brown University for a second application.

Sometimes, we could retrieve a sock by tiptoeing to the front hall, easing the door open, then loudly clinking the brass cover of the mail slot and dropping something through, so that Dudley would forget the sock and take off for the door. You had to be quick, though, and you needed to find the sock before Dudley caught on to the ruse.

I wanted my husband, daughter, and son to know that, of all of us, Dudley loved me best. So I devised this game: The four of us would sit on the den rug in a circle and—no gestures allowed, only voices—each of us called to Dudley, trying to lure him over. "Here, Dudley!" "Come on, boy!" It was noisy, all of us calling out to Dudley in our most seductive voices. But he always came to me. He made me feel like Miss Congeniality.

If my daughter or son had homework to do and did not want to do that homework, you could bet Dudley would emerge from one of their rooms fully dressed: sunglasses, baseball cap or straw hat, T-shirt, blue paisley bandana tied around his neck.

He did not like when our daughter or son gave him a bath. He did not like to go to the vet. He did not like to go to the groomer's for a haircut. He did not like the lavender bows the groomer fastened behind each furry ear.

Because there was no leash law then, Dudley roamed the neighborhood freely. Which means he roamed the streets freely. Which means he chased cars. Until a car caught him. He survived that, but limped badly the rest of his days. His bladder and bowels were never the same; eventually, he lost complete control of them. We tried to anticipate when he needed to go outside. When we missed, we cleaned up after him.

When it became really difficult for him to walk and he was in constant pain, I took him to our vet to be put to sleep. I held Dudley in my lap. He was quivering. He was whimpering. Did I mention he did not like to go to the vet? I was sobbing. It was the quickest the assistant at the vet's ever took us back.

I returned home from the vet's empty-handed. I picked up Dudley's food and water bowls from the brick floor at the back door, washed them, took the bowls and his leash, too seldom used, out to the tool shed. The only thing left to do was decide whether to write our daughter and son, both away at summer camp, or wait until they got home to tell them that Dudley was gone.

DUDLEY

STATE CHANGE

by Laurie Goldman Smithwick

I'm walking across

sharp coastal Bermuda grass

toward the pier.

The river,

motorboats,

tan summertime campers

everywhere laughing.

I just finished reading a letter

from my mom.

This was the moment,

the summer I was eighteen,

when I stopped being

a person with a dog.

SATCHMO

SATCHMO

by Lynne Fitzgerald

Satchmo, Satch, Satchee, Satcheeemo, Bubbaloo, little Buddy—our little boy-dog of many monikers has left us. With little fanfare and far too soon, this gentle, funny guy went out with a painless end, just as he deserved. We are grateful he outlived his prognosis. Grateful for every single extra day.

Satchmo came into our lives eight years ago as an eight-month-old puppy waiting out his rescue at a local Humane Society. From the moment we saw him we were smitten, even though his calm demeanor changed as soon as he was free of his kennel. I had never seen a dog bounce that high. Nor had I ever seen a dog move a crate the entire length of a kitchen from inside of it. We decided right there that that was the end of the crate, and he settled in nicely on a pillow with our other dog, Ella Fitzgerald, who would become his life-long companion.

Satchee never met a cat or a squirrel or a fast-moving little animal that he didn't want to chase. Even across roads. He loved bugs and butterflies and ducks and even bees—despite being highly allergic to them. He rarely came quickly when called, but he always came . . . eventually. When he was ready. He enthusiastically barked at mailmen and UPS drivers (particularly), but I suspect that they would have become fast friends had they been brave enough to meet him. He was always game, after all. They weren't. He was, at his core, a gentle little love pig with a big wide sloppy tongue that could clean a face in one go—and twice as fast if there was a hint of peanut butter. I can honestly say that he had not one mean bone.

He was overly enthusiastic in everything he did. When Satch ran full out, his back legs swirled like egg beaters, and he always lay froggy-style in the grass afterward, gnawing loudly on his favorite rubber ball. And despite the fact that he lived seconds from the lake, Satchmo never learned to swim—preferring instead to perfect the art of wading. This technique not only allowed him to cool off on hot days but served as an acceptable alternative to drowning. He also believed that greeting people at the door was his job exclusively, and he engaged in this task with LOUD enthusiasm—even in his final days.

Satchmo could also be a laid-back pacifist and was always submissive with dogs he didn't know—even to the point of Ella having to rescue him more than once. That said, he ruled the roost in our house, pushing Ella out of the way to grab a fallen morsel of food or to get the best spot on the bed or to steal the empty toilet roll that she had and he wanted. He loved carrots, Kleenex, sticks, toilet rolls, tomatoes, fresh summer grass, and peanut butter most of all. Oh, and the occasional lottery ticket. In truth, Satchee loved everything but skateboards and kale. And he so loved kids. I was always a bit sad that he came from a family of young boys to our house, as he was forever drawn to the sounds of kids playing and laughing across the yards. He also loved his Ella. He was gentle, loving, loyal, and sweet—and always forgiving of our occasional impatience and those days when he'd miss his walk. He was the true embodiment of a "good dog."

We loved him from the first moment we saw him, and despite his unexpected health issues, we would have rescued him again knowing how it ends. He had us at "woof."

So on a day we've been sadly anticipating for nearly a year, the house is suddenly too quiet. The mailman quietly comes and goes. Guests civilly enter and exit with little noise or fanfare. The squirrels in the backyard have a renewed nerve, and the dynamic of the house has changed forever . . . as it always does when a beautiful soul leaves.

I will forever miss the softness of his fur, the smell of his paws, the dome of his head under my hand, and his soulful brown eyes begging for just one more treat. So here's to a happy, funny, gentle boy who I trust is already chasing bees and squirrels with abandon. We are so sorry you had to leave us so soon. You were so loved, my beautiful boy.

ANNIE

GO, DOG, GO!

by Stephanie Whetstone

She was my first Internet romance. My only one, really. At first, I didn't tell my husband, Jeff, about her. He wouldn't approve. We had two small kids, after all—two and seven years old—and, yes, the seven-year-old wanted a dog, but we had no business getting one, Jeff said.

"But we have a fenced yard," I said.

"Steph."

I nodded. "You're right," I said, but continued to sneak glances of my girl on Petfinder. She was a coonhound, or at least part coonhound, and I have a thing for hounds. In fact, I had to search "coonhound" many times to find her.

Coonhounds are native to the mountains, like my family. They are singers and runners and working dogs. They are misunderstood like lovers in a country song. My girl was lean and beautiful, tan and black, small, with a pretty face and long ears. She didn't mean no harm. She didn't want to be a homewrecker.

"Let's just go meet her," I said. "Then we'll decide." To me, this meant what it sounded like, but Jeff knew better. He went anyway. We had both grown up in the country, both had dogs all of our lives until we moved for his graduate school, had kids, then moved back to North Carolina to a house with a fenced yard. In my mind, it was time. The kids needed a dog. So did I.

Annie was her name, and she was in a pen with her two brothers when we met. The way she looked at me, begging to be set free, there was no way I was leaving that farm without her.

If you've never had a hound dog, you must know this: they run. They are bred to run until they drop, to chase a raccoon and tree it, but leave it untouched for the hunters, who never shoot the raccoon. It's all about the chase. Annie would have been a champion hunting dog, but we tried our damnedest to make her a pet. We tried to teach her to sit, to fetch, to play with a ball. She wanted to run.

When you have a coonhound, it's best to be on friendly terms with your neighbors. Annie had a voice, and she sang whenever the mail came, whenever a car went by, and whenever a neighbor came up on our porch.

She also ran. It's the thing she most wanted to do, and she was fast. The "fenced yard" meant nothing. She jumped it the first day. We tried to add chicken wire to the top (again, it helps if you get along with your neighbors), but that only provided a new challenge. We saved up for a six-foot fence. That would do it, we thought. It did not.

Eventually, Annie's running became a spectator sport of sorts. Our neighbor Marcia stood on her porch and hooted with laughter as Jeff, the boys, the neighbor kids, and I chased Annie through the neighborhood like clowns let out of a tiny car. It was comical if you were watching instead of chasing.

All we had to say was, "Annie's out!" and the neighbors deployed.

"I saw her in Lizzie's backyard!" Chuck would say.

"I tried to catch her, but she went down the street that way!" Marge would say, pointing in the opposite direction.

Annie's favorite hiding place was under a house a few streets over, where skunks were nesting. Early one morning she made her run for it. Jeff and I, both clad in pajamas, ran in opposite directions. He had a package of hotdogs and followed his hunch. He was the winner! But how to get her out without riling the skunks? He crawled under the house on his belly and lured her out slowly with the hotdogs, then leashed her and dragged her home, waving to the neighbors along the way, triumphant. They shook their heads and waved back.

We live in New Jersey now, and though our North Carolina neighbors say they miss us, I doubt they miss Annie. Most of our new neighbors have never seen a hound dog in the fur. "What kind of dog is *that*?" they say. " A Vizsla?"

Annie's old now, and her eyes are clouded with cataracts, but she's still lean as a racehorse. "Isn't she too skinny?" the new neighbors say. They don't know that she's trained her whole life to run marathons, to race through the night. They don't know she was built for speed. If not for her timidity judging the depth of the stairs these days, you'd never know her age.

She still slips away from us every now and then when groceries are brought in, or the screen door is left open, and we still try to chase her, like fools. She has slowed a hair, but she still wins.

"She's no pet," Jeff says. "She's a wild animal." That's why I love her so much. She couldn't possibly be tamed, but she always comes home eventually, and sings at the front door until we let her in. She claims her spot on the couch in front of the fire and sleeps as if nothing happened, no doubt dreaming of running across miles and miles of unfenced fields, eyes again keen, legs fresh, finding the coon and running wild, singing for the pure joy of it.

Reprise

I am walking around the block in Brooklyn with Annie and a man stops me,

"Is your dog, okay?" he asks.

"Yeah, she's just old," I say. He nods, gives us a sad look, and moves on. It is winter 2020, and Annie is seventeen. Her hips have started to give. She can't see well, and she has a lot of accidents, but when we take her for walks around the concrete block, she comes alive. She can't believe her luck: the smells of New York City never sleep! It takes us forty-five minutes to make the rectangle, and we get to know the regulars: the Russian lady with the poodle, the young girl with the lab, the couple with the weimaraner. Annie is slowing down and we know it. Were we wrong to bring her to New York— so many steps and so little grass?

Then the pandemic hits and we flee to North Carolina, where Annie remembers the woods, and then to her favorite, the best-smelling place in the world, South Carolina. She revives there, sometimes leading a chase around the yard, running with a catch in her gait. This is the land of living things and soft couches. This is dog heaven.

It is where I imagine Annie is now, the ethereal version of South Carolina, now that she has finally left us. She saw our youngest back to college; he held her in his arms as the vet helped her find peace.

I still look for her when I come downstairs. I still think she is somewhere around, maybe just run off, doing laps around the neighborhood, forever and ever and ever, the best bad girl in the world, as any hound dog should be.

OPAL

OPAL

by Christine Dryden

We'd gotten a puppy shortly before losing an old, well-loved dog to a long life. The peacefulness of that passing was in sharp contrast to what we were about to encounter.

Life with a puppy is frenetic, with a household and routines routinely upended. And with Opal, life was a constant chase.

It was a bright January afternoon. I was working at my computer when a notification popped up on my phone warning of a loose dog in the neighborhood. Suddenly, the idea flashed through my mind that we could lose the wild puppy that had dominated our household for the last seven months.

Before I could pull the thought from my head, a child screeched into the house, breathless and frantic, screaming that Opal was out and they needed help finding her.

We hadn't yet gotten around to hiring a trainer to curb her tendency to dart from any barely-cracked door or gate and run like she was on fire. As a result, we had daily chases through the neighborhood. Oftentimes she started her run by scarfing cat food from the porch of our 100-year-old neighbor—an act that helped us get better acquainted. This constant darting positively infuriated me, and with my anger, my sense of dread increased as she grew bolder and more adventurous by the day. Her high jinks became more chaotic and farther-flung—one day she'd go three doors down, the next three blocks, then all the way to the border of our compact neighborhood.

But on this January afternoon things felt different, as she led us on an epic chase for what must have been miles. Six kids pursued her on foot, through creeks, over fences, and across a major city street in five-o'clock traffic. I combed side streets in the minivan trying to cut her off, trying to lure her into the car. My husband did likewise, shuttling the kids closer to the dog, putting them within reach over and over again before she'd zip away. Over and over again.

The expressions of terror on the children's faces as she scrambled between cars still haunts me.

I'll also never forget the face of our crazy dog that day—PURE BLISS. Her mouth gaped, panting, grinning. Her eyes were full of joy. She was bounding with excitement, galloping down the sidewalk. I've never seen a happier dog. She was clearly thrilled by the chase and the unfamiliar territory, and clueless to the danger she faced from the cars that raced by.

We weren't there to see her get hit or witness her stumble from the road. Kids were scattered around the block, running in her direction. I was a block away, waiting for a break in traffic. We all arrived at the scene a minute later to find her lying calmly on the sidewalk with a kind couple hovered over her, kids gasping—in disbelief that their pursuit had ended there.

"Someone better ride in the backseat with her," the gentleman said. "She might not make it to the hospital." My mind immediately rejected the notion. But he was right, and she did not. The sweet, wild creature closed her eyes cradled in the arms of the ten-year-old who loved her most.

The vets placed her on the table at the animal hospital and gave us time to stand staring and stroking and sniffling. All around us, their work quietly continued. We stood there until it was beyond awkward, then shuffled away. Riding home in the dark that had set in while we were inside, it was silent but for the soft whimpers of children.

JESSE

JESSE, MY FRIEND AND PROTECTOR

by JoAnne Macco

Three days after we brought him home, Jesse almost died. The four-month-old golden retriever wouldn't eat anything or even drink water. The vet said he must have swallowed something toxic. He gave Jesse IV fluids and sent us home. There was nothing to do but wait.

My kids and I sat with Jesse on floor of our enclosed back porch. I sat with him for hours, stroking his fur, knowing he was feeling miserable because he just lay there. I would have brought him into bed with me at night, but my husband, who only tolerated dogs, would not have allowed that. That night, I simply prayed that Jesse would live.

After two days, Jesse drank some water. The next day he ate some food. The next day he was a puppy frolicking in the backyard.

It was a few months later when my husband left our twenty-year marriage. I didn't see it coming. Looking back, it makes sense, but at the time, I was in shock. Devastated.

Through the challenges of being a single mom and two unhealthy rebound relationships, Jesse was there for me. Through the lonely years, Jesse was my most loyal companion. He was better company than any of the men I dated. Jesse didn't complain. He didn't lie. He didn't talk politics.

But he did love his walks. Long walks with Jesse eased my grief. Watching him run along the beach and splash through the waves made me smile. In the years when it was just me and my daughter, Jesse and our little dog, Marigold, went with us on vacations to the mountains.

Jesse was our protector. He was not the typical laid-back golden retriever, at least not with strangers who approached without proper introduction. That almost got him in trouble when he bolted through the front screen door and attacked a man who came into the front yard. He was an old friend of the family, but a stranger to Jesse, and Jesse bit him on the arm. Thankfully, the bite didn't do much damage, and our friend was relieved to know we had a protector in the house.

Fear couldn't get a foothold when Jesse was with me. We hiked through the woods every year on my birthday, just the two of us. We'd get a little lost on purpose to feel the sense of adventure and satisfaction of finding the trail back home again. Sometimes I longed for a human partner to share the trails. It had to be someone who loved dogs, of course. I knew Jesse wouldn't live forever. I prayed that if God was going to find me a soulmate that he'd come before Jesse died.

When Jesse was ten, my high-school sweetheart found me after thirty-nine years, and the timing was perfect. David had three dogs who he loved like family. He called them the Three Amigos. There was Doodle, the coonhound; Oreo, the spaniel; and Beep, the Australian shepherd mix. When the Three Amigos became my stepdogs and we had five dogs in our two-bedroom house, things were a little crazy. Walking together as a pack helped, and Jesse adjusted better than any of the others. Funny, he never had a problem with other dogs, but it took him a while to warm up to people. But he trusted David right off the bat, which was a good sign.

When Jesse was thirteen, his quality of life began to deteriorate. By summer his back legs stopped working. We managed to buy him a few more months with medication, injections, and acupuncture. David went with me to all the vet appointments, often carrying Jesse to and from the car. I was thankful to have a partner who understood. Jesse improved slightly for a while. On our pack walks, we tried using a towel to lift his torso, but the walks got shorter as Jesse got thinner. He lost ten pounds in his last year, even though we were feeding him more.

By winter, when Jesse was almost fourteen, he didn't want to get up, even to eat or go out to relieve himself. I knew it was time to say goodbye. Still, it was one of the hardest things I've ever done.

I asked the vet what gave me the right to end his life.

"It's not so much a right as a responsibility," the vet said.

I have to stop thinking about how after the vet gave him the second injection, the one that shut down his brain, Jesse's mouth opened, and his body tried to take a breath.

"Why is that happening?" I said as panic gripped my heart.

"It's only a reflex action," the vet said. "He's not feeling anything. He has no heartbeat."

"Does that happen often?"

"It does happen sometimes, but it's rare. He's a tough old guy."

"It's only a reflex," David echoed, trying to reassure me.

I wish I had known it might happen, to prepare for the possibility.

I had to remember that Jesse was too tired to even go for walks anymore.

I had to remember how, when I made the last call to the vet, Jesse's body was tense with pain.

I had to remember the trips we took to the mountains when Jesse swam in the lake and how he loved to run along the beach, splashing through the waves.

I had to remember how he protected my family and our home so well and what good company he was during my lonely years.

I now imagine Jesse pain free, with no worries, swimming and running to his heart's content. I look forward to hiking with him again on wooded trails, the adventure of getting lost on purpose, and finding our way home on the other side of the rainbow bridge.

I'm counting on it.

COQUILLE

DEAR OLD DOG

by Nancy Benjamin

Now the last and sweetest
of our retrievers
is suddenly old
as we are, too,
tiring faster
at times surprised
by things she loves
and can no longer do.

She stays close
beside our chairs
or at our feet
snoring softly
in sleep so deep
she doesn't hear
a knock, a doorbell,
a voice calling her.

She'd rather lie
on the dock
than swim out
to fetch a ball—
hard to stand up

with bones so sore
her tail thumps
when we come home.

Head on my lap
she seeks a caress
looks into my eyes
when I whisper
and wags her tail
understanding.
When no one is looking
we steal a kiss or two.

To think of life without her
by the bedside
at my desk
in the kitchen.
She walks with me
on beach mornings
wading where she used to romp—
dearer every day.

HENRY

I'LL NAME HIM HENRY

by Alexis Carreiro

Henry was the neighbors' dog, and I loved him. It was 1985, and he looked like Benji, but better.

He'd sneak through the bushes to sit with my little brother and me on our front stoop after dinner in the summer. We were convinced he knew when we needed to whisper our hopes and fears in his warm, floppy ears. "The neighbors don't deserve him like we do," we'd assure each other as we took turns hugging and kissing him. "He runs away all the time. They probably don't even know he's gone! If he was our dog, we'd know if he was gone." We lived off a busy street with a 45-mph speed limit, and his owners just let him roam around the neighborhood like a drunken toddler with no curfew. I was ten, and I hated that he wasn't our dog.

I could never understand why the kids next door didn't want to spend every waking minute with Henry. Why did they watch cartoons or go to a friend's house when they could have played with him instead? With Henry by your side, a walk in the woods became an epic adventure. Running through the sprinkler with him was a rain shower in the jungle. Cuddling in the grass was conspiring with a partner in crime. Time with him was magical, and he made everything more fun—something I desperately needed.

My parents' marriage was violently falling apart, but Henry kept me glued me together. I hated being trapped inside the house with them, so I'd sit outside with Henry instead. We sat face-to-face on the stoop, and he'd gently press his forehead into mine as my parents yelled at each other in the house. When they slammed the doors, he'd bark at them to stop. He spoke up for me when I couldn't; he knew what to do when I didn't.

Henry was more than just a pet. He was my protector and my safe place. "If I ever have a son," I thought, "I'll name him Henry." But I never did. And never did.

I was away at college when I learned that Henry had been hit by a car at the end of our old street. "Of course," I thought. "Of course." My biggest fear for him had come true, and to this day, I cry just thinking about it.

At thirty-nine I bought my first house. It was the fenced-in backyard that sold me, because I knew what that meant; I knew what it represented. Just as Henry had been my safe place, now I had one to offer in return. Two years later, I finally got a dog of my own. He'd been abandoned by the side of a busy road, and it took the rescue organization a few weeks to catch him. He was abused, skittish, and scared, but they were patient and kind and helped shape him into a friendly and very good boy.

Over the next few months the rescue organization fostered him and sorted through endless adoption applications until they found mine. This was my opening line: "I'm a college professor, a published author, a small business owner, and a public speaker. And I will spend the rest of my life trying to make him happy." (No one else stood a chance. Step aside, kids. I've been preparing for this moment my entire life.)

On January 1, 2016, Smiley McGoldenWolf came to live with me, and it's the best decision I've ever made.

I couldn't save Henry even though he saved me, but I was able to save Smiley McG. And every once in a while, when we're sitting on my back porch pressing our foreheads together, my heart overflows with the unconditional love that only a dog can summon—then I close my eyes and whisper into his warm, floppy ears, "Hi, Henry. You're home."

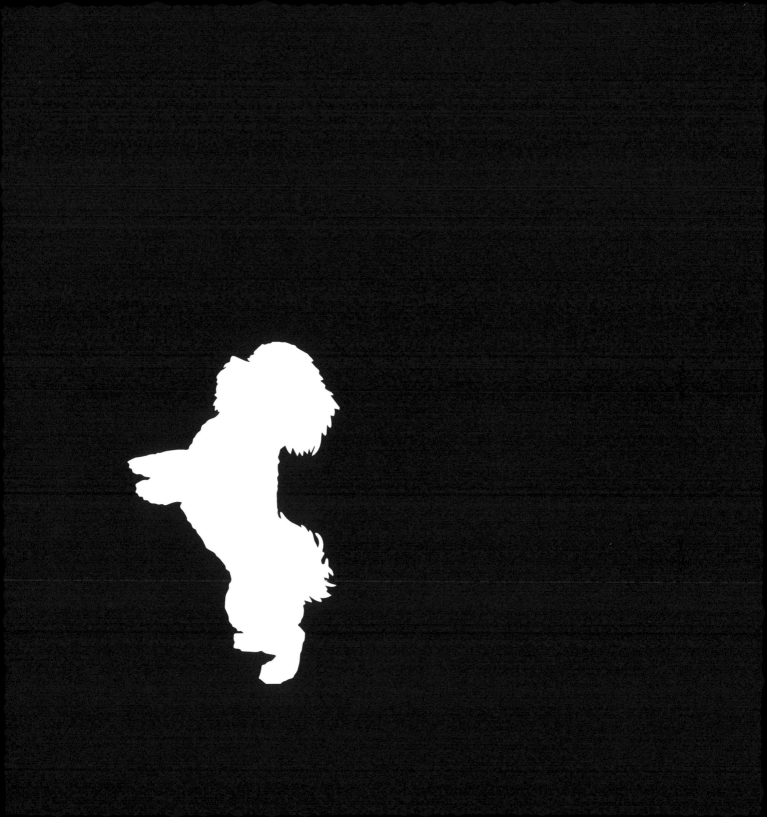

ZACH

ZACH

by Susan Hilger

His name was Zach, aka my heart—all of it. I adopted this small, twenty-pound mix of dachshund, beagle, and Boston terrier, in 2000 while I was living alone, working full time, getting a degree, and being a mom to a sixty-pound mutt. The vet guessed he was a few years old. Two weeks before, he'd been hit by a truck and thrown into a building. He'd been with the vet since the accident, and they were ready to send him to a new home.

Zach started out pretty rough around the edges. When I first brought him home, it was as though he'd had no indoor life. But it didn't take long for him to take over my little condo, while also taking over my heart.

About a year later, Tim entered my life. And Z quickly took over his heart too.

One day we noticed Z squinting in one eye. It looked painful. He'd already endured a lot—kidney disease, multiple herniated disks, losing and gaining a new packmate—and despite it all, he never looked dejected. Until the day we noticed the eye.

It turned out Zach had glaucoma, which is incredibly painful. The vet explained that the best thing to do was to remove the eye. Both Tim and I decided that we couldn't take the guy's eye just yet, and we took Z home, where we administered four different kinds of eye drops twice a day, for several weeks. Zach had good days and not-so-good days, but in the end he showed us what we needed to do—and we scheduled the surgery.

The day of the surgery we impatiently waited for news. After a few hours, the vet called. The surgery was complete—and successful. Zach did great. We picked him up a few hours later.

When we got him home, he was groggy but seemed pretty chill. All we wanted was for him to be OK, because he was Zach—our wonder Zeagle! Within a day, he was back to his old self. Yes, he was one-eyed, but he was the happiest we had seen him in a while. It was obvious he had been hurting more than we knew. It wasn't long before he and his sister were tearing through the house, barking and playing.

Zach lived happily for another two and a half years.

Z was more than a dog to us. He taught us so many lessons about how to love—and we're both forever grateful. And as much as we miss our Z-man, we live his lessons every day.

LANGSTON

MY DREAM DEFERRED

by Barbara Presnell

That Sunday if you'd come to my house, you'd have found me under the bush in the backyard, where I was combing my dog, pulling out handfuls of old summer fur and stuffing it into a bag.

 I'd spent a lifetime combing his thick, half-chow hair. As he aged, he grew impatient with me rolling him onto his back or to this side, then that side, or yanking the tender hairs of his belly or tail. But this time, he didn't try to hop up and chase a squirrel or push me away with his wide feet. Something was wrong.

Over the previous few days he'd steadily lost energy. And other than the small bowls of rice and beef broth that I cooked for him, he wasn't eating. I could comb all I wanted and he wouldn't run away.

As I combed, I spoke. "I'll bet this feels a lot better," and "You're going to look so good when I'm finished." When I did, he rolled his big, milky brown eyes up at me as if to say thanks, before blowing out a tired breath and laying his head back down.

My Langston. I believe the animals we need come to us when we need them most. Soon after moving to a new town thirteen years before, I was still adjusting and evaluating. One evening, as I pulled in from work, a gangly, untamed black puppy bounded down our driveway. I took to him immediately, but he was wearing a collar and, I reasoned, was too beautiful *not* to be owned by somebody.

But despite our efforts, no one stepped up to claim him. We named him after Langston Hughes. He was my "dream deferred"—the dog I always wanted, I told my husband. He was the little black dog my mother made us give away thirty years ago, and he'd found me at last.

But he was wild. He wouldn't listen. He wouldn't walk on a leash. He jumped on children and adults. He could run as fast as a thoroughbred, his thick black hair breezing from his face. He ate *everything*: the back porch, the yucca plant by the gate, the dryer vent—twice—and the doghouse I built for him.

Night after night, I sat with him on the back porch and pleaded, "If you don't calm down, I can't keep you." He'd lick my face, smile, and then bury his soft head in my lap.

But he was smart. He quickly learned to sit, lie down, and shake hands. "Kiss, Langston," I'd say, and he'd hop up and lick my face every time.

Despite his intellect, every chance he got, he'd sneak out the gate and run wildly through the neighborhood. The more we chased, the faster he ran. So we'd wait, and eventually he'd come home. Meanwhile, we'd listen to people in the park next door scream as this big black animal—gentle as a lamb—came bounding toward them, his large incisors smiling and that bear-like fur on end. I'd have screamed too.

Whatever critter crossed our backyard was dinner. Possum, squirrel, bird, snake. Even my kitten Stuey, for which I finally forgave him.

On the occasions he came inside the house, chaos erupted. When he wagged his tail, he wagged his whole body, knocking over tables and toppling shelves. More than once, we chased him through the house as he tore after a cat that was ricocheting off walls and couches to get away.

But I could sit on the back porch and wrap my arms around him when I especially needed him. He'd hug me back, tucking his big black head into my lap or shoulder, his warm body next to mine. He'd sit with me as long as I needed. He'd let me talk about anything. He'd walk and walk and walk as far as I needed to walk.

When we brought him home from the vet that Monday evening, we knew we were bringing him home for the last time. With slow steps, he made his way to the back fence, curled himself underneath his favorite bush, and lay down. Every thirty minutes or so, I walked out and checked on him, rubbing his soft head, talking softly like so I had many times before. Of course he'd roll his brown eyes up, and then close them. Happy.

Around eleven thirty that night, I opened the back door and there he stood. He'd mustered the energy to walk to the door one last time, where, every night of his life, I stepped out to tell him good night. This was our last.

I know this is just another dog story, and my Langston was just another dog. But he was my dog, and it's my hand holding the leash that's now dangling empty.

Our animals come to us when we need them. They teach us unconditional love and selfless giving. They teach us joy and laughter, patience and forgiveness.

They teach us all they can, and then, when we are ready, they let us go.

RUBY

RUBY

by Callum Saunders

There are many stories I could tell you about Ruby. And many different ways in which I could tell you those stories. But after several weeks of gestation, I kept circling back to one driving force: the only way to truly tell Ruby's story is through the lens of an old photograph. How a visual image triggers a written story is less an irony and more a confluence of currents.

And as those currents started to become words flowing from my fingertips, it became clear that I wasn't writing "a story" about Ruby, but more how her story continues to move through me today; how I see, navigate, and sense a world of memories all around me whenever I am back at the family home. Perception, space, and time dance with each other in mysterious ways.

And the flow of Ruby's energy continues to be felt today.

I found a box of photographs the other day. Real, physical photographs, glossy, tactile, and wonderful. Even the most innocuous of memories feels somehow more meaningful when committed to physical print. One of these photographs was slightly bent in one corner, where it had clearly been squashed into the box. I picked it up and looked upon it, instantly transported back to a time and place as the beauty of what it captured drew me in.

The landscape was the Sussex Downs, right behind my mother's house—up high on chalky downland that has curved and undulated for millennia. I am lying prone on the grass, giving a lower sense of perspective. The midpoint of the photo is the horizon, where the warm, pallid earth meets a pastel sky. My three siblings are there, walking up hilly tussocks toward an eternal July evening. I can feel their motion and hear their chatter right now.

In the foreground, plodding after them, is a black shadow with four legs. To say she is shapeless is not intended as factual, but a reflection of her age: the glossy contours of a Labrador's prime long gone.

There is no specific symbolism behind this particular photograph, no occasion beyond the very scene it captures. It merely framed a moment when four siblings had managed to come back home together at the same time. I remembered feeling as if we had the Sussex Downs to ourselves on an evening when heaven and earth seemed fused as one.

And it's this singular image that evokes everything Ruby was to me. Her loyal following and slow gait, her subtle yet constant presence, her inquisitive and loving eyes. Her happiness just lying somewhere, being with her family, and taking in the world around her—as though she existed on a time continuum slower than our own. Even today I often see parts of my own personality in hers: the humanity of a dog is never to be underestimated.

The English poet Edward Thomas penned a poem titled "The Unknown." Three lines have always struck me:

The simple lack of her
Is more to me
Than others' presence.

I look upon the garden on warm summer days and gaze longingly at the same patch of grass where she lay in her final years. Silent, content, and immovable, she was a black rock: steadfast and true, in the humming, pulsing rhythm of an English garden in August. Her ashes are buried right behind it and feed a rose we bought for the occasion—a variety named Ruby (what else)—but it's that patch of warm, baked earth, rather than the blooms her ashes send forth every year, that sings to me and speaks to my soul. "The simple lack of her is more to me than others' presence."

At the family dinner table, I can almost feel her head upon my thigh—Labradors and the eternal optimism of a tidbit from the table. How strange it is that she has been gone all these years, and yet my soul still has the muscle memory to outline the shape of her head with my hands, to still know the very weight of that old head as it plodded down upon my leg.

As I move through the family home, there are tens of different spaces—worn patches, scratches, chewed baskets—that still tell her tale to those who knew her and can read the inscriptions. Her story is not reimagined and retold in our minds. It's there in physical space, while time dances around it.

"The simple lack of her is more to me than others' presence."

As I look at this photograph now, I can feel her heat in dusty whispers.

My Ruby.

BELLA

A MUTUAL RESCUE

by Beth Dozier

Bella wasn't supposed to live past the age of two, if she made it that long. Together, she and I refused to accept that reality.

As a puppy, she was abandoned in a park, dropped there by someone who likely suspected what I would later learn: She had grave health problems.

Our bond was indelible right from the start. Bella wanted to be with me all the time, and because I worked from home, we were rarely apart. She never needed a leash. In fact, she never left my side, unless I declared, "Go, girl. Go!"—her signal to run, leaping like a gazelle over bushes, fences, and even other dogs, all while never leaving my sight.

It's difficult to articulate why Bella was so special, but I'll try. She thought she could talk—literally vocalizing softly in a Chewbacca-esque bark when I asked her questions. There was also the range of emotions she seemed to demonstrate with the ease of a human being—from love and excitement to understanding, jealousy, vindictiveness, and disappointment. She could read my emotions better than any person ever had, always nudging her head under my hand or leaping up to cuddle when I needed a friend.

It was as if Bella knew that our bond would extend her life.

When she was nine months old, she stopped eating, and her powerful personality faded. After several fruitless trips to a veterinarian who insisted my sweet girl was getting thin because she was "just a diva" and a picky eater, I found a new vet and demanded that the staff check her liver. That's how Bella was finally diagnosed with hepatic encephalopathy—which means blood was being pumped around, but not through, her liver. As a result, Bella's blood was filled with toxins. She was a very sick puppy.

The vet recommended I try a few human medications but told me I should still prepare for the worst. Dogs with her condition, the vet said, rarely live past age two.

I began managing her disease with daily treatments, prescription food, and lots of love. Soon after, she began to recover—eating, loving, and leaping once again.

After I got married, Bella moved with us to Manhattan's Upper West Side—right across from Central Park, where she was free to be off leash every morning. Each day began with Bella running circles around the other city dogs, taunting the poor pups by bounding right over them just when they thought they'd caught her.

But the New York winters were tough on Bella, and at age three, her liver disease once again reared its ugly head, and she stopped eating. Our veterinarian said that I should prepare to put her down, but Bella's big, dark eyes told me—begged me—to do more. She wanted to live.

Refusing to accept that a creature with such a vibrant soul could have such a short life, I sought out Manhattan's premier animal hospital—which happened to be one of the best in the country. I carried my emaciated best friend through the doors and said simply, "Please fix my baby."

Bella lived five more years, almost to the day. Five more years of continuous medications, prescription food, and cajoling to manage her condition. But most importantly, five more years of unconditional love, entertainment, and companionship—the likes of which I have never known since.

Those additional five years were a precious, unexpected gift. And I never took a single day for granted.

As our little family started to grow, I was convinced that Bella sensed I was pregnant. As soon as I found out about the baby, Bella started carrying a stuffed animal with her to the park. It was as though she wanted to carry a baby, too. She would leave the toy at the park entrance, do some running and leaping and playing, and then retrieve her "baby" for the walk home.

Once our daughter was born, Bella became devoted to her as well—growing quite protective. She never let her tiny human out of her sight. If I lost track of my daughter on the crowded playground for a split second, all I had to do was follow Bella's gaze. She would even climb up on the playground equipment to make sure her toddler was safe.

Every morning after my daughter awoke, Bella would hop in bed with us to snuggle, usually with her head on the pillow in her typical "I'm not really a dog" fashion. She was too polite to wake me up herself, but once she heard my voice, it was time to love on each other. She never missed a morning cuddle session—not even on the day she passed.

One week after her eighth birthday, Bella became sluggish. I thought it was just her liver disease demanding a different antibiotic. Over the years flare-ups had been routine; they typically meant that her body had developed a resistance to the current regimen. But later that day, she jumped up to greet my mother-in-law and immediately collapsed. She couldn't move. Her eyes took on a glassy, faraway look.

I carried Bella through the animal hospital doors, weeping as I begged the staff to save her. They took her immediately to the emergency room. I refused the waiting room and followed my baby.

For hours as doctors performed tests, I comforted her, wept over her, and told her—and myself—that everything was going to be OK.

I knelt at her side, her body splayed on the cold, metal table. She nestled her head in my hands as I whispered words of love and reassurance, her eyes peering into mine for strength.

As her condition worsened, she lifted her head and placed it on the opposite edge of the table. I thought she might want to be alone in her pain, and I wanted to honor that. But when I left for a moment to talk to the doctor, she tried to lift her uncooperative body to follow me. She wanted her mama there. And I desperately wanted to be with her.

After the battery of tests, I learned that the problem wasn't her liver. It was cancer. A hidden tumor had ruptured, leaving her bleeding internally. After years of managing her health, there was suddenly, horribly, nothing I could do, except help her transition.

While I waited for my husband to arrive, I held my Bella, whispering in her ears that she was more than a dog; she was my best friend. And I understood that now she had to go.

Her breathing slowed, and her eyes began to close as she accepted, finally, that we had to part. Remarkably, when my husband arrived, she used her last bit of strength to lift her head and wag her tail.

The will to live, and the need to love and be loved, powered Bella her whole life. This strength helped her overcome her myriad health problems to the amazement of every veterinarian we ever saw. It allowed her to be energetic, even as the cancer grew inside her. But for the first time, her strength wasn't enough.

As the doctor prepared to put her to sleep, I held her cold, wet nose against mine and told her soul to wait somewhere for me. I felt her last breath push against my face.

I was torn apart with grief, hot tears accompanying a pain that was deep and palpable. But above all, I am grateful. Bella taught me about the sanctity of life. She taught me how to love more deeply and without expectation. She taught me how to fight for what's important. She made me a warmer, better, stronger person.

I thought I was rescuing her that fateful day we met eight years earlier, but the truth is that we helped each other live life to the fullest.

MOONSHINE

A DOG CAN CHANGE EVERYTHING

by Tony Tallent

We were backwoods kids, and we had backwoods dogs. We had the kind of dogs that chased cars up the gray gravel road that ran between our small houses and a clear stream along the hillside. Our dogs lapped water from this same stream and hid in the wild tufts of grass beside it. They waited with tempered patience for us to call their names. They waited for the next growling motor to come up the road. They waited, always ready to dash.

This road brought pickup trucks and souped-up cars creeping or flying past us. It was a gray line of worry, this road, for the kids who had car-chasing dogs. The sound of an accelerating motor would send us calling their names. We wanted to keep them near us, petting their mottled coats, begging them to stay on our porches where they'd be safe. But we knew you can't hold back a dog with a mind set on chasing a car. These backwoods dogs had a brave tenacity, like the kids who ran beside them through rocky fields skirted by woods.

Our dogs had names like Rex, Brownie, and Red. There was Charlie, King, and Brandy. And there were all the nameless dogs who would wander into our yards. We'd feed them what we could find, though adults warned us about feeding any animal that wasn't our own. They'll wind up staying, they said. And many did. Some stayed for years and some for only stints of time, just long enough for us to give them names and think they'd always be there.

Sometimes we'd wonder what types of dogs they were. We'd reason one was mostly collie with a mix of something else. If a dog was taller and had pointy ears and a long nose, we'd say he was likely a police dog and must be really good at guarding things. They were mixed-breeds, as some might say. Others would say they were mutts. We loved them anyway, and our love blended with the wonder and worry that backwoods kids carry around with them.

These dogs came from all over the place—from houses tucked back along the branches of North Carolina mountains, from my parents' coworkers at the furniture factory, and once from the town dentist, who was desperate to give away a litter of growing pups. We took them in and treated them well, at least from the perspective of a kid who didn't know dogs. Even the muttiest of them needed more than a place on the porch to keep them safe and well.

Our lives with these dogs were punctuated by loss. Dogs left out in the cold. Dogs carrying one litter of pups too many. Dogs that went missing without explanation. Dogs chasing cars, or dogs that didn't move fast enough from the gray gravel and a growling motor.

These dogs were left for us to find, to cry over, to bury in grassy patches near the worn-out road. We always wondered why the car just kept going. The driver must've known what had happened.

Sometime between my sixth and seventh birthday, my parents brought a new dog home. It was one of the rare times when there were no other dogs roaming in our yard or resting on the porch. This dog was different from most we'd known. His coat was sleek, short, and as dark as a starless sky. He walked with a trot that made us imagine he'd been trained. His ears stayed pointed and never drooped, and his tail had a perpetual curl that kept him in an almost feline pose—graceful and aware. This was not a backwoods dog. He was the type of dog that could prance right onto the set of a show we were watching on our black-and-white television screen. And yet, here he was, in our backwoods world. Our dog now.

My parents named him Moonshine. It sounded like a noble name to me, and I thought they'd given it to him because of his coat, so dark it could catch the very light of the moon. I didn't understand there was any other type of moonshine. We knew he had to be a special breed, maybe a purebred. My sisters and I guessed he could have been a miniature pinscher. Or maybe he was a corgi, though he was solid black and too broad to be one breed, too tall to be another. Whatever breed he was, we all agreed: he's a sure-fine handsome dog.

Moonshine, this stocky little dog, became a pleasure in our somewhat pleasureless lives—an unexpected pride we shared. He wasn't the kind of dog to run through the fields with, but he would trot along beside us. And in this way,

Moonshine put a new trot in our routines: we called his name as we ran up the road from the school bus, brushed his black coat with the tips of our fingers, and anticipated the time to feed him. He was changing our minds about dogs, and it felt like everything could change because of it.

My father bought Moonshine a red collar. This common action was a large gesture in the world we knew. Backwoods dogs seldom wore collars. Moonshine's collar along with his own food bowl on the porch signaled this sure-fine handsome dog was winning the simple tokens of being a part of a family.

One weekend my mother and father had their photographs taken with my aunt's instant camera. They wanted Moonshine in the photos with them. In my grandmother's backyard, my mother halfway knelt beside Moonshine and gentled her arms around his neck. She didn't look at the camera but instead looked down at the dog, who was perfectly posed, ears perked, eyes looking straight forward. My father wanted a photograph of Moonshine by himself, and encouraged him to sit on a line of gray cinder blocks as if it were a stage. The photo was snapped as my father sidled away from the dog, his long arms reaching down to pet Moonshine, to say *Good boy, sit still for the picture*. Only a smudge of my father's outline and Moonshine's black silhouette made the photo. The rest was a blur of dirt and rocky bankside, cinder blocks, and the sliver of red collar around Moonshine's neck.

The photographs, including the almost-indecipherable one with my father, were placed in a family photo album. Moonshine, beside my mother, and the blur of my father reaching out to him, stayed there in the upper-right corner of one of the yellow gummed pages covered in the clear protective film meant to save images forever.

On Saturdays, we took one of our only regular family outings. We drove out of the cove down the steady decline of the gravel road to the grocery store in town. My sisters and I had to stay close to the grocery cart as my parents moved through each aisle—my mother insisted. We'd sometimes slip a bag of potato chips from the cart for the drive back. In the trunk of the car, packed into the brown A&P grocery bags, there were bright red-and-yellow cans of dog food for Moonshine. It would be time to feed him soon.

We called his name as we carried the bags of groceries up the porch steps. *Moonshine!* Holding on to the porch rails, running from the front to the backyard, we shouted, *Moonshine!* Why would a dog not come when it was time for his supper? Our voices reached across the fields above and below us, our friendly calls now tinged with worry. *Moonshine?*

Dusk was setting in when my father walked around the curve in the road below our yard. His arms grasped something we couldn't see clearly in the waning light. As he moved closer we knew he'd found Moonshine. We called his name out of pure habit. There was silence when we saw that his dark body was limp in my father's arms.

In the farthest corner of the porch was the red metal wagon my parents had given me two Christmases before, its black handle twisted to one side. My father placed Moonshine in the shallow bed of the little wagon. We ran to him, my mother holding us back from touching the dog as we looked to see breath rising from his small, stout body.

A car got him on the road, my father said, and he told us how he'd found Moonshine huddled in the tufts of grass. The tears that came were of both loss and disbelief. Here was our dog. It was way past his feeding time. He wasn't moving. Everything was changing.

Someone turned on the porch light. It was getting dark. Still, we hovered around the wagon, hoping to see Moonshine move enough to make us think he'd be all right. My father finally reached down and picked up the dog. On the metal of the wagon's bed where his head had laid there was a thick liquid that had seeped from his mouth. My father put him back in the wagon and covered him with a towel. Moonshine stayed in the wagon all night as we tried to sleep inside.

By morning, the wagon was empty, and we knew Moonshine was gone. My father had buried him in a lump of field near the road. My sisters and I stared at the empty wagon. The thick liquid spot left there had puckered and formed a small circle of cracks in the red paint.

We did not know how to miss a dog. We put the cans of dog food away to help us forget. If we called his name out of habit, we'd stutter our way into talking about something else.

When the weather grew warmer, I found a half-used can of gold spray paint that'd been left outside. I pulled the red metal wagon to the backyard and sprayed the paint all over it until there was nothing but a hint of the red left to see. Still there, in the bed of the wagon, was the puckered circle, now gilded with the cheap spray paint—this small cracked circle, a mark of pain, a mark of missing.

There would be other dogs, too many other backwoods dogs. There had to be a sure-fine handsome dog among them. One that could change everything.

LUCY

LUCY'S GIFT

by Laura Boggess

As I was finishing up the last chapters of my book, Lucy Mae was dying.

I was writing a book about joy, and about the value of play in the grown-up life, and there I was—wracked with grief over the slow death of the family pet.

This dog had grown up with my two boys. For ten years she nuzzled their faces and chased after their feet. She was supposed to be around for a few more years; she was supposed to keep me company when they left me to go off to college.

But one day, out of nowhere, she had a seizure and never completely recovered. In the daytime hours I would write my book and read the words out loud to her as I'd always done—watching for some recognition in her sweet empty face. In the evenings, my two boys and I would take her for shuffling walks, covering only a sliver of the distance we used to walk in half the time.

Everything slowed, and time felt like the cold hand of death reaching under our door.

In truth, nothing in my life felt right. I was realizing the dream of writing a book, but I felt more alone than ever as I watched the man I love battle clinical depression. He slipped deeper into despair as I helplessly stood by. Meanwhile, our eldest son had become involved in a relationship that we didn't approve of, and one night after music lessons I had to rush our youngest to the ER with a panic attack.

Our once secure and happy family was splintering all around me. What used to be my safe place was becoming a place of uncertainty and fear. Who was I to write a book about a joy-led life? The words I'd penned just a few months before when life was blissfully happy seemed to mock me.

And now Lucy Mae was dying. This dear, innocent creature, who had brought so much sweetness into our lives and had brought us together in so many ways, was paying the price of a broken world.

How could I possibly write about joy in the midst of such sorrow?

As her time drew to a close, Lucy Mae rewarded us in new ways. It was one of her last days, and we were walking. She struggled with each step but, oh, how she wanted that walk. Watching her, my two teenage boys were silent. And the deep places in my heart spilled over with pity for our girl.

"Seeing her this way," I said, "makes me love her more. Even though it hurts, all I want to do is hold her and let her know we're here."

The boys nodded, and my youngest picked her up. I watched how tender he was with her, how careful and kind.

"I'm glad for Lucy," he said, tears threatening. "I wouldn't trade our time with her for anything."

I felt something new stir in my chest—a bigger kind of love, a love that doesn't run in the face of pain. And I felt it then: joy. I felt how sorrow carves out room inside our hearts to feel deeper, to love deeper, and enter deeper into relationship—not only with those we are joined with in life on earth, but with something bigger.

And when I sat down and typed out the final chapters of my book, I was companioned by this rich knowing of how sorrow and joy walk hand in hand. This is why we give our love when it would be easier to give up and turn away.

Because love is greater than sorrow. This lesson was Lucy Mae's final gift to my family.

And I wouldn't trade that for anything.

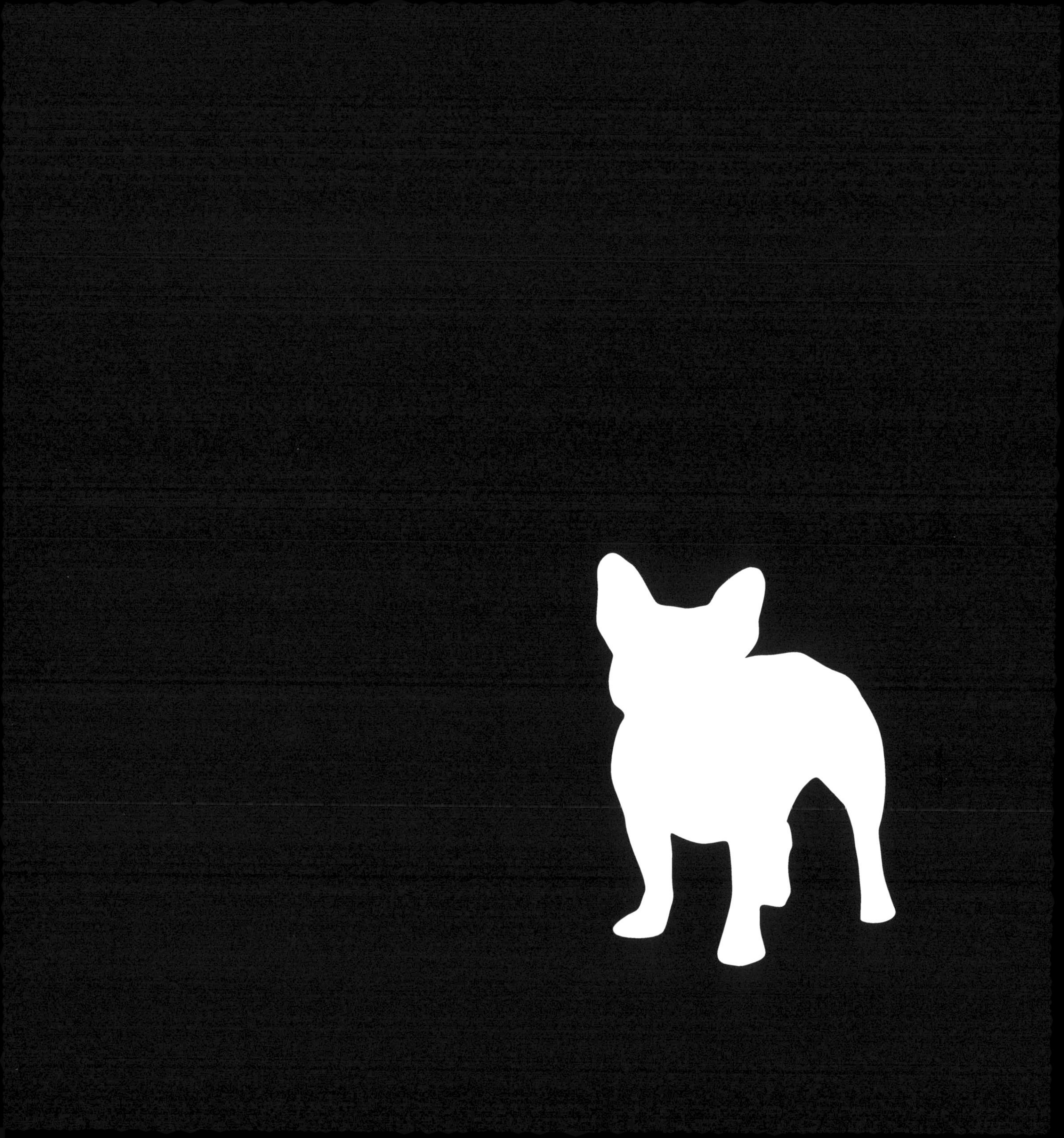

FRED

OUR OLD DOG

by Tommy Tomlinson

He just showed up one morning. It was early November 2001, a couple of months after 9/11. We were all walking around with holes in our lives. I went out to get the paper and there was a white ball wriggling at the end of the long driveway. The closer I got, the faster he wagged. I looked at him. No collar. I looked around. No people. He followed me back to the house.

I picked him up and took him in the bedroom, where my wife was sleeping. Alix! I whispered. Look! She put her glasses on and noticed a couple of things I didn't—the puppy was bloated from worms and crawling with fleas. That's nice, honey, she said. Let's take him outside.

Our yard didn't have a fence, so we took him across the street to our neighbors while we figured out what to do. As we walked back to our house I looked back. The puppy was right on our heels. He had squeezed through the gate to follow us.

We had a dog.

We settled on the name Fred. Fred's a solid guy. Fred's your buddy.

We took Fred to puppy training a couple of times, but the main thing he learned was that people have treats in their pockets. And when we'd take him on walks, he'd turn around every 20 feet and beg for a snack. When he wasn't begging, he was sniffing. He had some hunting dog in him—among other things. And he was a scent hound to the core, plowing his snout into bushes and down holes, checking out the crotches of every creature he met. This was not so charming when we had company.

We kept him in the garage while we built a fence. Fred basically ate our garage. He chewed the drywall. He chewed the attachments to our Shop-Vac. We kept a plumber's snake in a five-gallon bucket. One day we came home and found the top half of the bucket chewed off, the snake sprawled on the floor, Fred dancing in the garage with glee. He ate about as much plastic as he did dog food in those days. His favorite snack was poop from the Canada geese who hung out at our little pond. He snapped up the turds like Tootsie Rolls. We'd steer him away from the droppings, but he'd always find one we missed. Never once got sick.

Those geese at the old house used to torment us. They'd poop all over the walkway between our back door and the carport. One morning Alix saw them gathered outside the garage and decided a dose of Fred might scare them off. She hit the garage door opener and Fred took off. When the door lifted enough for Alix to see, she saw two things: One, Fred had in fact scared the geese silly—they were taking off toward the pond. Two, the geese had brought their babies. Fred had a gosling in his mouth.

Alix chased him around the yard, hollering at him to drop it. Fred thought this was a fantastic game. After a minute or two, Alix ran back in the garage and grabbed a dog treat. She showed it to Fred, and he instantly dropped the gosling. It took off running to find its family. Fred had cradled it in his mouth the whole time, never biting down. We knew then we had a gentle dog.

Sometimes I'd roughhouse with him and he'd grab my arm with his teeth, a million years of wild dog battling a thousand generations of breeding. He never clamped down. Far as I know, he never hurt another living thing.

Here's what I remember most. I'd let him out every morning to roam the backyard, which was as deep as a football field. He'd go way back there and sniff around the edges of the brush while I stood by the house and watched. After a while I'd whistle and he'd look up. I'd dig a treat out of my pocket and hold it high where he could see.

In three strides he'd be going full speed, ears blown back, eyes wide with joy, every muscle in perfect sync. He barely touched the ground. He never stopped on time so he would go flying past and slam on the brakes, scrabbling in the dirt like a cartoon. Finally he would make it back to get his treat, his tail spinning like a helicopter blade.

Years later, on his good days, sometimes his tail would spin like that when he saw us. It lifted our hearts off the ground.

Fred had fears we never understood. He cowered at the sight and sound of trucks and, for some reason, white vans. He ran away from children. He was about two months old when he showed up at our house, and we always wondered what happened to him in those two months. Nobody ever put up signs in our neighborhood looking for him. We think he got dumped in the street, or escaped a bad place. He sure seemed grateful to be with us.

He had some Lewis and Clark in him. Every so often he'd get loose and take off, exploring the neighbors' backyards. I'd chase after him. He'd look over his shoulder at me and trot just out of reach. Finally we figured out a trick: We'd get the car and drive to where he'd wandered. As soon as he saw the car, he'd jump in. There was nothing he liked better than a car ride. He'd stick his head out the back window, jowls blown back, nostrils pumping with all the smells he was taking in. After a while he'd prop his front paws on the console between our seats and lay his chin on my shoulder. A dog can love you in a way that caves in your heart. It can also leave a lot of drool on your shirt.

When he was three we moved to a new house which had a little yard and a front porch and lots of people walking around. It took him some time to get used to this. Fred was an introvert. Of course he'd sniff another dog's butt. That's dog law. But some dogs are alpha dogs, and Fred was an omega. A 55-pound weenie.

I think Fred was born for the North. Every year he wilted a little more in the summer, and every year he perked up in the fall. Snow days were his favorite days. We had a big storm at the old house one day, and he dove in and out of the snow like a dolphin. We spent a year in Boston and it snowed 60 inches that winter. He'd bound through the park across from our apartment and come home with a snootful of frost.

That Boston year, we drove up to Maine one fall weekend and took him to the beach. He never was much of a water dog, but he loved chasing gulls, wading in the ocean, and trotting in the sand. He was seven years old by then—a middle-aged dog—but he high-stepped down the beach, ears thrown back like he was a puppy. If you're good to a dog, pretty much every day for the dog is a great day. But that one might have been the best. We rubbed off as much sand as we could and piled him in the back seat, and he slept all the way home.

It was one of our best days, too.

When Fred walked into our lives, we didn't think we had time to look after a dog. But when it's something you care about, time bends and stretches. Somehow we had the time to take him for walks and keep him fed and clean up his messes and just hang out together. He never was well-trained, but was a skilled communicator. His go-to move was the heavy sigh. Sometimes Alix and I would be in bed, talking through something important, and all of a sudden from the corner of the room would come this long and deliberate exhale of profound boredom. No matter how serious our conversation was, it always made us laugh. *Wrap it up*, he was saying. *It's sleepin' time.*

He also won over our families. Alix's folks are not especially dog people, and my mama has been scared of dogs since she got bitten as a child. But they welcomed Fred into their homes. My mama even started tossing him little bits of bacon in the kitchen. When she found out he was sick, her advice was to give him some bacon. To be honest, that's her advice in a lot of situations. It's pretty good advice.

It's been weird to see Fred get older. For the first few years of his life, he pulled us down the street. Then he walked by our sides. At the end, we were the ones up ahead of him.

When he started getting really old, it didn't register with me right away. I'd yell at him for not eating his supper, or not wanting to go on his morning walk, or eating some random thing off the ground. I'd take him outside on beautiful nights and he'd just stand in the yard and look around. It got me really frustrated until I realized the problem: I was mad at him for dying on us.

It was about then that Alix and I tried imagining life without Fred. He was with us 14 of the 17 years we were married. We knew it was coming, but thinking about it was tough. It was our hope to remember the lessons he taught us:

Always make room for treats.

Sometimes you should wander off and see the world.

Explore things with enthusiasm, even if you're shy.

Any day might be the best day of your life.

Fred passed peacefully as the sun went down on an autumn Thursday. Alix and I were by his side, along with the same amazing vet who had cared for him since he was a puppy. We told stories and laughed and cried like children.

He had a good last few days. We discovered right near the end that he liked tuna fish, and he must've eaten half a tuna's worth. (Yes, Mama, we also fed him bacon.) The food perked him up. In his last weeks, he didn't have enough strength to take his normal walk to the end of the block and back. But the day before he died, he pulled us down there and then another whole block. On his last day we took him on one more car ride. He watched out the back window as we drove him through the streets he knew so well.

Nearly every night for 14 years, one of us let him out before we all went to bed. We'd spent so many nights standing in the cool air on this street we love, staring at the stars, listening to the neighborhood owls, or just watching Fred prance around the yard and catalog the smells. He brought us those moments and a million more.

I didn't know what to do on that first night without him, so I walked out in the yard and stared at the stars and thanked him again for coming into our lives.

I don't know your thoughts on the afterlife. One thing I hope is that we'll be able to sit down and have a conversation with Fred. Have him tell us why goose poop tastes so good, where he really liked to be rubbed, whether we did right by him at the end. Make sure he knows how lucky we are that he showed up in our life one day.

My other hope is that up there, we're all young and strong again. I'd love to watch him run.

Reprinted with permission of *Charlotte Magazine*.
Photo by Logan Cyrus.

KINSEY

KINSEY

by Todd Jones

We were about three months into our very brief stay in Pittsburgh when we decided to go out for ice cream on a chilly January evening in 1999. On the way, I stopped by a liquor store while Stephanie went into the pet store a couple shops down.

When I caught up with her, I knew immediately that ice cream wasn't happening. There was this very young, very hyper schipperke bouncing around in one of the kennels inside the store . . . and Stephanie was lost. Even though we realized that pet-store dogs were cruelly bred and buying one went against everything we believed in, schipperkes and Stephanie go back a long way. And there was no denying the connection these two ladies had. So we justified the purchase as a rescue and took her home.

Her name, Kinsey Robbin, evolved from two things: Kinsey from the main character in Sue Grafton's mystery novels (I was working in the legal investigative field at the time, and Stephanie was a fan of the books), and Robbin because we never got ice cream that night (and "Baskin" sounded dumb as a middle name).

Kinsey was a blessing to us, and amusement for our three cats. We moved back to Seattle about six weeks later, and we found that Kinsey enjoyed cross-country travel, marking every rest stop along the way and loving the journey.

 At one point we became convinced that because Kinsey had been around the cats so long, she thought she was one. She meowed. She perched on the back of the couch. We eventually got another dog (Indiana) to bring her back to canine reality. They became fast friends. Kinsey never liked any of the other dogs she came to know the way she loved Indy.

We have fostered a lot of dogs over the years and adopted many others. Kinsey was always the undisputed alpha over all of them. She outlived all the cats and two of her canine brothers—including her beloved Indiana.

Kinsey loved being at school when Steph was working as a trainer. She liked being in the car. She loved chicken fingers and reindeer sausage and any pasta smothered in cheese. When she was young she would dance and play and run like nothing else, and in her older years she loved wandering in the yard, letting the sun warm her bones.

Her last couple of years were tough on her, but she managed—and we managed. She became incontinent, and she had been living in a pen of towels and pads for about a year when my job relocated us to Connecticut, so Kinsey got one more cross-country adventure. We even revisited most of the same rest stops just for her. Back east, she got another new yard to explore. She was still contained, but she got more time with the people and the pack who loved her. She went blind. She went deaf. Despite always being alert and hungry for a meal, she lost a lot of weight. We can't begin to understand what made her hold on for so long, but as with everything else in her little world, Kinsey did what she wanted, and we never questioned it for a minute.

On September 5, 2016, she told us she was ready. She got one more bite of chicken before her appetite truly disappeared. She took one last walk in the backyard with the fresh air blowing through her fur. One last soak of sunbeams. Kinsey got one more sniff from her brothers and sisters. One last bath. One last scratch behind the ears. One last kiss goodbye.

The next day she slipped away from us and to wherever all those who went before her were waiting, hopefully with a hot bowl of macaroni and cheese ready for her to devour.

SHANNY

SHANNY

by Karaleah Reichart

It was one of those breezy spring days that we didn't get too often in Wisconsin. The sun was shining, and the grass was swaying in the fields on the drive to the farm. I was going to take a look at a cocker spaniel puppy that was for sale. Apparently, nobody really wanted her because she wasn't up to "breed standards," whatever that means. This was way back in the days of newspaper ads, and when I came across the classified, I figured, well, it couldn't hurt to go for a nice drive and check it out.

I pulled into the driveway and curled around a long road toward the barn at the back of the property. A nice lady came out to greet me. I noticed out of the corner of my eye that her son was playing with something that looked like a squirming bundle of black-and-white fluff. When I shut the car door and turned around, that little fur ball suddenly had big floppy ears and a little stubby tail that was going back and forth a million miles an hour. It was looking right at me, dead in the eye.

And that was it, folks. It was all over. I never had a chance.

I always called Shanny my number-one baby, because she really was like my child before I had children. Her full name was Miss Shenandoah O' Shannahan, because why not? She deserved a fancy name, and she knew it.

I dressed her in all the finest fashions, served her the best cuisine, presented her with the comfiest beds, and always gave her the most fun toys that Walmart had to offer. And tennis balls? Everywhere. You couldn't walk around my house without tripping over balls.

As she grew, Shanny collected more nicknames. When my son was young he couldn't pronounce her name, so Shanny became Shoo Shoo. Once, when she was in her teens, Shanny was irritated with me for going to work and decided to spread an entire roll of toilet paper all over the house. After that her nickname became Satan's Spawn. She particularly enjoyed scrubbing her butt across the floor, and thus she became Scoota Boota.

Shanny was so important to me that she is forever immortalized in the annals of history, as she is listed in the acknowledgments section of my dissertation as a "significant source of emotional support."

Because she was.

She was my shadow. We went everywhere together, both flying on planes and driving across the country and back twice. We went so many places together that I started making a collection of photos of her peeing at tourist spots.

Until we both got sick.

I started getting tired in the afternoons, and when I finally got around to taking my temperature, I discovered that I had a low-grade fever. The fever didn't abate, and with increased pain in my joints I decided to see my primary-care doctor. She promptly sent me to a specialist, and they did blood tests and X-rays and other scary medical things. I remember thinking, *What exactly is an autoimmune disease*? They sent me home with some medication and their best wishes.

I started planning days around my fevers. I would get up early in the morning, intent on finishing all my writing and research by three o'clock, when the fever would come. Shanny would sit beside me on the couch whenever I was in too much pain to do anything else, and we would watch TV shows together. *Celebrity Deathmatch* was our favorite.

Then one day I noticed that Shanny wasn't herself. At first I thought that maybe she was just in a slump because I wasn't as active as usual. But on days I felt well enough to take her on walks, she'd struggle to breathe. She was gaining weight, despite not eating much. I took her to the vet and they did blood tests and X-rays and other scary medical things. They ultimately determined that her thyroid was failing, and it was affecting her heart.

I never shed a tear when I was diagnosed. But when Shanny got sick? I cried nonstop for a week.

I started her on medications for thyroid, fluid retention, and blood pressure to heal her heart, although the vet said her prognosis was "guarded" because of the damage already done. I'm pretty sure that's the medical equivalent of standing on the fence so you don't have to take sides. It's what they tell you when they think the dog is probably not going to make it out alive, but if they do, they can say they knew it all along.

But damned if that dog didn't keep going.

She began dropping all that fluid that I mistakenly thought was fat from not taking walks. With the weight loss, her personality rebounded. She had more energy and started to get her twinkle back in her eyes. She was happy again, and she was healing. And because she was happy and healing again, I started to feel happy, too.

Shanny lived for more than a decade after that episode. When she started going blind at age five, she quickly learned how to find her tennis balls by listening for the bounce. When she went deaf at age ten and couldn't hear the bounce anymore, she felt the bounce through her paws and then used her nose to guide her the rest of the way. She remained passionate about the quality of her toys, her bed, and her food.

Then one night when she was thirteen, she refused dinner. I knew that something was very wrong.

It was a rainy Saturday, and our regular vet was closed, so I called an emergency vet and rushed her over. I was greeted by a small woman in a white lab coat with her name embroidered on the lapel. I remember contemplating the absurdity of holding firm to the theater of medicine, particularly in a thunderstorm in the middle of the night with a dying animal. She could have shown up in jeans and a T-shirt and I would have been cool with it if she knew how to save my dog.

But she couldn't save her.

Shanny had a malignant tumor the size of a large orange on her liver. She hadn't shown any symptoms. But it was crystal clear from the x-ray that my number-one baby wasn't going to make it out of this one alive. The vet said she had maybe a week left, if that.

I sat alone crying in this strange vet's office, contemplating whether to take her home for one more night, and how utterly impossible it is to say goodbye to a friend that's been at your side for thirteen years. I called friends and family to let them know. Then I made my decision.

Shanny put her tired head on my arm, and we cuddled like we used to when she was a baby. She looked up at me, and maybe I imagined it, but for a moment, I saw those bright little puppy eyes that had grabbed my heart thirteen years before. Without the wonky thyroid, or the bad retinas, or the soundless ears, or the liver cancer, or the old age. Just peace and love and bliss and . . .

And just like that, she was gone.

I put her ashes in a box on a shelf with her picture, right next to my dissertation. She's a part of our family that used to be here but isn't anymore—like grandparents and great-uncles. To this day, whenever I see a black-and-white cocker spaniel, my first instinct is still to shout, "Hey, look, it's a Shoo Shoo!"

And it makes my heart smile, every single time.

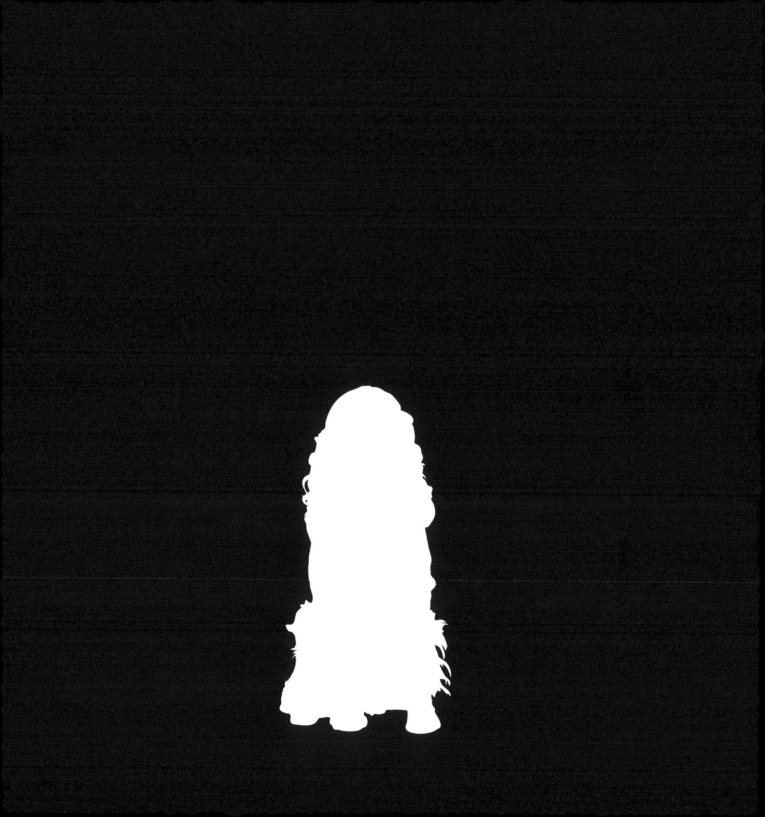

BOOMER

A SMALL DOG AND A TINY TREE

by Jason Fox

Boomer was no George. At least, that's what my parents informed my older brother, David, and me upon hearing our preferred nom de pooch for the newest member of our household.

Though the memory, now thirty-five-plus years removed from the incident, comes wrapped in more than one layer of time-spun gauze, I do believe David and I merely wished to honor one of our favorite television characters at the time—George Jefferson. Obviously. And while it has since become popular to give your dog a more human-sounding name, our society was not yet so onomastically progressive. Thus, our folks thought other people—or perhaps the dog himself—would be confused by such a sobriquet, and so we opted instead for Boomer. Who was also a bright star of the 1981 TV season, but at least he was an actual dog.

A mutt of indeterminate terrier origin, the Dog Barely Known as George was a pound puppy. Boomer arrived the day after my dad and brother had surrendered our first family pet, Sunshine the cocker spaniel, due to his increasingly violent and territorial nature. And so Boomer bounded into a household that was equal parts sadness, joy, and Gaines-Burgers. But, brief naming crisis notwithstanding, he melded into the family swiftly and completely. He was, by any definition, a good boy.

I am of the firm belief that all dogs are special merely for being dogs. I will not explain this statement, as it is either blindingly obvious to those who agree, or impossible to comprehend by those who regularly purchase Fancy Feast. But as far as dogs go, Boomer was rather, well, ordinary. He wasn't big on tricks, save for attempting to catch Orville Redenbacher's finest as tossed nightly by my popcorn-loving dad. He didn't have any particularly goofy personality traits, unlike my current dog, Fletcher, who adopts the kids' stuffed animals as his own and yet never eats them. Sure, Boomer would jump on my bed in the morning to wake me up if need be. But at a svelte eighteen pounds, he wasn't exactly entering the realm of Marmadukian hilarity. He was just, as I said, a good boy. And he was mine.

But then. Then there was the tree.

As far as the outdoors were concerned, Boomer was happy to contain whatever exploratory urges he might have possessed to the backyard. Roughly sixty-five by fifty-five feet of befescued glory, our backyard would never be mistaken for something akin to acreage. But it was cordoned off with a chain-link fence that permitted Boomer leashless excursions to hunt his two archenemies: squirrels and the Big Brown Monster, aka the UPS delivery truck. Beyond these sporadic—if wholly expected—bursts of energy, his relationship with Creation was fairly sedate. Until that day a year or two into his tenure when he decided to go off script.

"Hey, Jason, come here. What's that hanging from Boomer's mouth? It looks like a coffee can. Is that . . . is that David's tree?"

Not quite, Mom.

For by the time we spotted Boomer nonchalantly trotting across his domain with a coffee can full of dirt dangling from his mouth like the world's worst inverted lollipop, he had already consumed most of the tree, a ponderosa pine sapling that my brother had acquired at school in honor of Arbor Day and subsequently planted inside a coffee can.

What had possessed this otherwise mild-mannered mutt to devour an eight-inch conifer, we would never know. He certainly didn't volunteer the information, nor would his actions over the years yield a single clue, as he never once repeated this behavior in even a tangential fashion.

Perhaps the prickliness of the pine needles passing through his lower GI tract proved enough of a warning. Perhaps he misheard the famous treble clef mnemonic and thought that every good boy deserves firs. Or perhaps he simply wanted to let us know that while wackiness was not his raison d'être, wackiness could, at any moment, ensue.

It was a Friday in the spring of 1995 when we finally had to let Boomer go, as his kidneys failed and his eyes dimmed. I can recall that day more easily than even those of (much) more recent vintage. My parents adopted another pound puppy, Scruffy, the very next day, because that's what you do when you can't imagine life without a dog. As for me, I suppose that was when I finally grew up. Sure, I had graduated college the year before, landed a job, and moved out on my own, but to say goodbye to the dog of your youth really is to say goodbye to childhood.

At least Boomer didn't make me grow up too fast. A good boy to the end.

GYPSY

SQUEAKY SHARK

by Jennifer Merlich

During the summer of 1996, my father was at his wit's end trying to figure out how to help me through a badly broken heart. In a move that still amazes me to this day, he presented me with a puppy. He thought it would be good medicine for me as I tended my battle-scarred heart. He was right. The puppy was a tiny poof of a thing, literally fitting in the palm of my hand. If not for the impossibly large brown eyes peeking out, you'd never know there was an actual dog under all that fuzz. But there she was—a wisp of a pup who took my breath away and stole my heart. It was love at first sight, and I named her Gypsy Rose.

Gypsy came bursting into my life like a whirlwind. Instantly precious and quite precocious, she was a joy and a challenge all at once. She was fiercely independent, yet almost co-dependently attached to me, and it was immediately apparent that she and I were soulmates. Looking back on it now, I can so clearly see how she was basically me in dog form. Wild and unsettled. Fearless yet fragile. Stubborn and strong-willed, but prone to whims and frequently flighty. Prissy, high-strung, and more than a little manic, Gypsy was a full-throttle little girl who craved love and yet sometimes shrank from it too. Whether by nature or nurture, Gypsy was a reflection of me at that tumultuous phase in my life.

Gypsy loved her toys, but the day I brought home a small, plush shark with a squeaker inside, Gypsy was instantly smitten. She snatched squeaky shark out of my hands, jumped onto the couch, and began to suck on the toy like a baby would a pacifier. It was both ridiculously endearing and odd at the same time. Sucking on the shark seemed to soothe Gypsy, like a child is soothed by sucking its thumb. I can still remember the sucking sounds she'd make and the way her big brown eyes would grow heavier and heavier as she suckled herself to sleep. Soon, squeaky shark was just an extension of Gypsy—it was as much a part of her as her tail or her paws.

During the weeks following Gypsy's passing at the ripe old age of sixteen, squeaky shark became a sort of pacifier for me as well. I clung to it those first nights when the loss of my sweet girl was almost too much to bear, clutching it in my hands curled against my chest as I slept. Holding it close soothed me, as it had soothed her for all those years. And although I no longer cling to it in my sleep, it does still reside in a place of honor on my nightstand.

When my new puppy came along after Gypsy passed, the night-and-day difference between the two dogs was startling. Where Gypsy was always excitable and predictably danger prone, Phoebe was calm and serene, with confidence and grace that was surprising in such a young pup. Where Gypsy would manically chase a ball for as many hours as I would throw it, Phoebe was content to meander along, stopping to smell every flower along the way and every blade of grass underneath it.

But however different they were, they both shared a fascination for the little squeaky shark. From day one, Phoebe was drawn to the toy, despite it being safely tucked away on my nightstand out of her reach. For a very long time, I kept it away from her, mostly due to her proclivity for eviscerating all things plush. The squeaky shark was sacred to me, and as much as I loved my new little charge, I couldn't bear to share this one thing with her.

As Phoebe grew older and time softened the jagged edges of my grief over losing Gypsy, I started to let Phoebe play with the shark on occasion. And as I did, I began to see the dilapidated little toy through new eyes. I came to view it as a legacy Gypsy had left behind for me to cling to during the saddest times, and for Phoebe to toss wildly into the air and catch during the joyful ones. It had seen so much love in its lifetime with Gypsy, as was evidenced by its missing left fin, its frayed teeth, and its threadbare dorsal fin, and it finally felt right to allow Phoebe to enjoy it as well.

Now, every time I look at the tattered little toy, I recall the lines from *The Velveteen Rabbit*, describing what it means to become real: "You become. It takes a long time. . . . By the time you are Real, most of your hair has been loved off, and your eyes drop out and you get loose in the joints and very shabby. But these things don't matter at all, because once you are Real, you can't be ugly. . . . Once you are Real, you can't become unreal again. It lasts for always."

That silly, squeaky shark: made real by my beautiful, wild Gypsy Rose. And now, occasionally allowed supervised visits with my precious little Phoebe Grace. But still, more often than not, residing on my nightstand within arm's reach just in case the fierce and fragile, strong-willed but now only occasionally manic girl I am today needs to reconnect with the free-spirited wisp of a girl that Gypsy was.

ZOE

ZOE

by Sarah Brett

I didn't see Zoe when I turned onto the gravel drive to my parents' lake house. She would usually be there to greet visitors, tail wagging, and with a tennis ball in her mouth. I had just made the three-hour drive home from college to visit my father, an increasingly common weekend trip since he had been diagnosed with cancer two months earlier.

When I think of Zoe, I can't help but think about our house there on the lake. Zoe would always be the first in water as if to lead the way and make sure everything was safe for us. She would pause, leg deep, and look back toward us to see if we were coming. Then she would turn and bound in. It went this way all throughout middle and high school, spending the long summer days cooling off in the lake with countless tennis balls retrieved from the water, Zoe always at the ready to lead us in.

As I walked into the house, signs of Zoe were everywhere, from the torn screen door to the worn edge of the sofa and a half-chewed tennis ball on the floor. I found my father uncharacteristically sitting at the kitchen table instead of in the workshop or his favorite easy chair.

"Got some bad news, Sarah. Zoe passed away this morning. She just walked in the kitchen and fell over. I made a little bed out of some towels here and held her. She didn't seem to be in pain, she just kept breathing slowly for an hour or so until she stopped. She was old, you know . . ." He trailed off, his voice breaking. He said she seemed content that someone who loved her was there with her in the end to hold her. She knew it was time and could let go.

My father said he went ahead and buried her in the backyard that afternoon before I arrived. It was one of his final acts of independence before his cancer became too much and he was confined to a wheelchair. I imagined him holding her with his big hands, the contrast of calluses from his years in the factory against Zoe's soft fur.

The next time I came over, I found my father lying on the floor. "You mother was out, and I didn't call anyone because I knew you would be here soon," he explained as I lifted him back onto his bed. I noticed he kept one of Zoe's worn tennis balls on his bedside table. We knew it wouldn't be much longer, but Dad was determined to be strong until the end—fighting and refusing to give up.

I looked outside at the spot where Zoe was buried. Leaves covered her grave. She loved to dart into the piles of leaves we would try to rake, hiding her head while her tail wagged furiously. Now, with my father's cancer occupying everyone, the leaves were just left to be scattered by the wind.

The day my father died, I couldn't make it back from school until after he'd passed. When I arrived, my mother described being at his bedside, holding his hand as his breathing slowed and finally stopped. I was glad he had someone beside him so he wouldn't be alone. He knew it was time and could let go, just like Zoe. Even in her final act of dying, it felt like Zoe was leading the way—always the first one in the water.

Zoe was a comfort to my family, especially during my tumultuous teen years of raised voices and slamming doors. She was there to calm our frayed nerves and bring us together. I like to think that the strength she showed when she passed helped my father find his own strength when the time came.

I raked the leaves off Zoe's grave and placed her worn tennis ball on top of it, then we scattered my father's ashes beside her spot overlooking in the lake. Dogs can teach us how to love and how to be loved. They can teach us how to live our fullest lives, and they can teach us how die when the time finally comes.

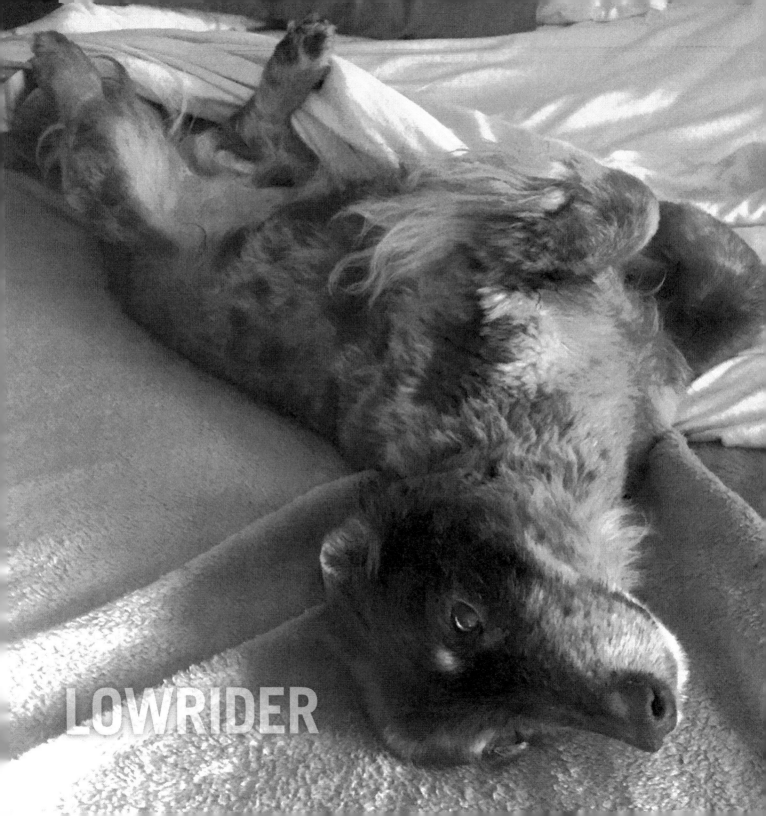

LOWRIDER

MEMOIR OF AN ELDERLY DACHSHUND

by Lowrider and Rachael Ikins

When they adopted me I was the smallest.
There were bigger sisters and brothers. People
gave me toys. Oldest Sister took them all. She had
such need. I could smell it. I contented myself
with a throw pillow.

When the taller siblings created a forest of legs,
teeth beneath the butcher block, I chose
the couch in the front room. The back rested against
a picture window. I used to climb up there. I dragged
my pillow. As I watched the world go by and barked,
I pulled the stuffing out of my pillow's carcass.

I dragged the corpse to my crate every night.
Big Sister's crate held so many toys, when she shifted
she squeaked. I loved my quiet pillow-skin.

Sometimes Mom stuffed it and sewed it shut. I think
she liked the process, my eviscerating pillow.
Her repair, gift for me again. She liked that it was mine.

We moved. Sister and Brother left us. I was the only dog.
Uncle Mike came over with a present for me. Mom told him
I never played with toys. I surprised her when I grabbed
the duck plush, shook it hard enough to make
it crinkle and quack, to break its neck.
I killed my duck again every homecoming, after car rides.

One day we adopted Little Sister. She was smaller and shorter
than me. She barked. She peed on Mom's belly. She embarrassed me.
They gave her lots of toys: pink bears, orange doggies,
rubber balls, toys that squeaked, rang, or chirped.
She is very good at eviscerating them. Within a day usually,
plastic squeaker silenced, white guts on Oriental rug. Mom gave her
a duck of her own. She likes my duck. I tried to hump her. She growled.
When we roughhouse, I always win. We don't live in the house

with the sofa under the window anymore. Or the country cottage,
Or in the faraway city where Mom's heart beat way too fast.
We live on the third floor with a balcony. We are home.
I watch Little Sister break my duck's neck.
I curl in my soft bed next to Mom's chair. I guess it is
her duck now. I pretend not to care.
Stupid duck.

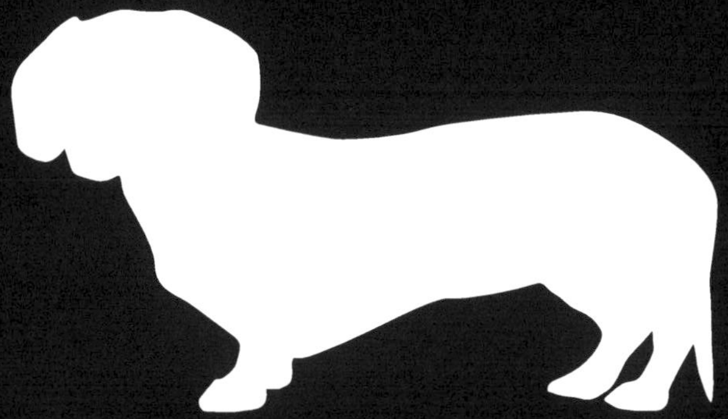

PHOEBE

PHOEBE, DAUGHTER OF HEAVEN AND EARTH

by Elizabeth Richardson

The first time I saw Phoebe, she was lying on a cot in her kennel at the county shelter where I volunteered. Other dogs were jumping and barking, but Phoebe was quiet and calm. I knelt to look through the wire mesh.

Phoebe gazed at me with dark brown eyes, her eyebrows white above one eye and gray above the other. Her fur was mottled with random splotches and patches of gray and black, with a generous peppering of white. Blue merle is the name for her coat, but in Phoebe's dim kennel, I saw no hint of blue.

My husband, Michael, and I started the adoption process, but we could not bring Phoebe home until she was spayed. It was time to pick a name. I hurried home to consult my primary source for dog names, *The Oxford Classical Dictionary*. A name jumped off the page.

PHOEBE, a Titaness, daughter of Heaven and Earth, wife of Cocus and mother of Leto. She is thus grandmother of Apollo (Phoebus) and Artemis. But her name, "the bright one," is not infrequently used for the moon.

The first two weeks at home, Phoebe proved what I tell everyone who adopts a dog from a shelter. You cannot be sure of what dogs are like by how they act at the shelter.

I never heard Phoebe bark until she came home. At three o'clock in the morning she started barking. For two solid weeks she barked and paced most of the day and part of the night. Phoebe did not do bad-dog things like chew on shoes, and she was immediately pals with Artie, our Labrador retriever. In most ways she was perfect. Yet I cried every day for the first two weeks Phoebe lived with us, because she never stopped her worry-like barks.

The more she barked and paced, the more agitated I became. The turning point came when I flopped down on a couch, exasperated. Phoebe came and plopped down, too—not beside me, on me. At that moment I realized I was part of Phoebe's problem. My agitation fed hers.

On the couch we both sighed our way into this realization, and into a pattern. I sat. Phoebe nestled in my lap.

I could almost hear her say, "Please sit with me. Stay."

"Yes, Phoebe, I will stay with you until your last moment on earth. Will you help me be still?"

Morning and evening Phoebe nudged me to remind me it was time for quiet, time to sit or lie down together. Often Phoebe lay near my legs and draped her tail over my ankles. Her tail was her glory. It looked like a huge quill pen, stuffed beyond measure with feathers, long soft hair flowing to the call of gravity.

Phoebe's body was not compact like some Australian shepherds. She looked as if a different breed had imparted a few inches of length. Curious, I sent off a DNA test, which revealed Phoebe was a collie/golden retriever mix. The golden retriever accounted for her long body and full flowing tail. Some collies have blue merle coats. I never tired of gazing at the patterns and hues in Phoebe's coat when she lay next to me.

Our closest, quietest times were just before sunrise and again before sunset, the liminal time when heaven and earth meet in the blue hour. We loved the evening blue hour, when the sun pulls his direct light beneath the horizon, allowing blue to charge the air. And in the morning, when the moon is sinking to her half-day's rest, the bright one giving way to blue.

Phoebe was at ease in these transitional times. She never seemed completely of this world, perhaps because the world had instilled fears in her. When Phoebe came to live with us, beneath her neck the fur was thin and the skin irritated. Our veterinarian concluded that she had a yeast infection, likely from a damp rope tied around her neck. She was scared of loud noises and terrified of thunderstorms. My heart broke when I imagined Phoebe tied to a doghouse or a tree and left to weather storms. No wonder she loved to rest next to me, safe. Inside.

Sometimes our morning quiet time ended while the world was still steeped in darkness. When I headed to the barn around sunrise, Phoebe would lie on her dog bed on the screened porch and watch me. When I finished in the barn, I sat near her when the sun was about to top the trees, near the end of the blue hour. Phoebe's coat of black and white and gray was transfigured blue. Phoebe, the bright one.

Phoebe and I loved quiet, but we also enjoyed activity, especially walking in the mountains. Many times we hiked on Roan Mountain along the border of North Carolina and Tennessee. More often we sat on the deck of our mountain home and looked up toward Roan Mountain, watching the sun tinge the mountain red toward sunset.

We also stared at Fork Mountain, which rises below Roan. Along a short stretch of Fork Mountain's ridge lies a meadow, constant in its place, changing in its colors. The meadow marks passing months as surely as a calendar, turning its grassy pages from yellow green to emerald, then russet, and finally the brown of winter's rest.

Years passed, and Phoebe and I kept our promises. For almost fourteen years Phoebe reminded me to be still. I stayed with her until the last moment of her life.

In her final weeks, Phoebe increasingly showed signs of pain. She looked miserable. The last morning, she collapsed on the floor and looked at me as if to say, "I can't do this anymore."

I told her, "Honey, you don't have to do this anymore."

That afternoon we took our last ride. Before we left, I clipped a few tufts of Phoebe's fur, a keepsake. Under the dim lights of our veterinarian's treatment room, Phoebe's fur was black and white and gray. As Phoebe drew her last quiet breath, I stroked her fur and remembered our blue hours.

Twenty days after Phoebe died, I sat in church near the end of an evening service, listening to the piano postlude. I gazed at a stained-glass window rich in blue. The air outside radiated the glass, casting it ultramarine. Heaven and earth intersected, and for a moment I dwelt in the in-between place. I felt something soft and flowing around my ankles, the sensation of Phoebe's magnificent tail. Phoebe was present, the bright one, daughter of Heaven and Earth.

CHESTER

CHESTER

by Marisa Rosenfeld

He was an afterthought that rainy November day, the Friday after Thanksgiving, 1988.

We'd closed on a new house a few days earlier and decided to move during the long weekend. I was leaving my apartment, and Michael was leaving his condominium. We'd bought the house together before we married.

I had hardly anything to move at the time, as I'd previously moved from Brazil, and my belongings were mostly in storage. I owned a sofa bed and TV, along with some silverware and dishes I had bought when I arrived. And, of course, my piano. The movers brought my stuff to the new house, then I waited an eternity for Michael to arrive. Finally, as day turned to night, Michael showed up holding his dog, Chester. I had totally forgotten about the dog.

Because we moved on a rainy day, the poor thing had gotten soaked and looked pitiful. Chester was half poodle, one-fourth Lhasa Apso, and one-fourth dachshund: furry, with a long body, and some air of nobility and duty. He wasn't good-looking anymore, he was blind, and he had bad habits, like peeing in the house. He was very shy and guarded, we suspected he'd been abused by Michael's son and his friends.

At first, Chester rarely got close enough for me to pet him. Regardless, I took him for walks, which he liked, and practiced patience with him. I discovered that he liked to play with tennis balls, and that helped our bond grow. But there was distance between us until February, when Michael left for a long trip—leaving me and Chester alone.

I started speaking to him in Portuguese and trying to teach him little things. and slowly but surely, Chester started warming up. By the time Michael returned, Chester and I were just about friends. Then my parents came to visit and, much to my surprise, Chester and my dad had an instant bond. Dad said that he and Chester had two important things in common: they were both old and blind. Also, Dad took naps after lunch every day of his life, and Chester would nap next to him on the floor.

Mom walked Chester during the day while I worked. It became apparent that he enjoyed walks with me or my Mom more than with Dad or Michael because we had firm hands. He felt secure with us. During their visit, Mom got sick and had to go to the ER. While she was recovering, suffering from pain and fever, Chester never left her side. Whenever she got up, he would follow her. That touched her deeply.

I used to buy whole chickens and make a sort of "chicken soup" for Chester: liver and gizzards, with broth and carrots. No words could do justice to how much he loved this soup. When my parents went to Pittsburgh to visit my brother and his family, Mom called one day and asked me if I had made Chester his chicken soup. "Really?" I asked. This from the woman who wouldn't let us have a dog as children.

Things were steadily improving between Chester and me. I had proof of his love one day when Michael's adult daughter came to visit. Their conversation quickly escalated into a fight over money. At one point things got really awful, and I said, "If you want to talk about money, you are welcome to talk about it outside." At that moment Chester leaped into my lap and cuddled with me. From that day forward, we were good friends.

In April of 1992, I went to Rio to visit my parents. The trip had already been scheduled when my father fell ill. Just before I left, Chester started acting strange. At times, I would find him sitting in the driveway or on the deck, sniffing. He sniffed up and down and in different directions, as though he was looking for something.

While I was in Rio, Michael called to tell me that Chester had disappeared. He figured that the dog had found his final resting place in the woods behind our subdivision. During the call, I cried in front of my ailing father. Dad was concerned and asked what had happened.

"Chester went to the woods to die," I said.

Without missing a beat, he replied, "Men should do the same."

A couple of months later, my father died. It was a consolation for me to think that he and Chester might be together somewhere on the other side.

INDIGO

INSIDE A DOG

by Jenny Boylan

I took her picture last year, one sparkling autumn day, as she stood on our dirt road waiting for me. There was a bright-red maple leaf on the ground.

This fall, I held that photo in my hands as the tears rolled down. Eva Cassidy was singing on the radio: "But I miss you most of all, my darling, when autumn leaves start to fall."

This is the season when columnists write stories about lives that came to an end during the year and remember small acts of grace—those gifts that cannot be asked for, only received. Here's mine.

My sons were twelve and ten in 2006, and our family had been through a wrenching couple of years. And yet, we'd emerged on the other side of those days still together, the four of us plus Ranger, the black Lab. Our lives revolved around that dog, and one another. But we worried that Ranger felt puny when we weren't around. Sometimes we arrived back at the house to hear him howling piteously. It was heartbreaking, his loneliness.

Then, someone emailed us about a dog named Indigo. She'd had puppies a few months before, and now she needed a home. Were the Boylans interested?

The Boylans were. And so Indigo joined us, as Ranger's wingdog. When she first stepped through the door, her underbelly still showed the recent signs of the litter she'd delivered. Between the wise, droopy face and the swinging dog teats, she was a sight to behold.

She had a nose for trouble. On one occasion, I came home to find that she'd eaten a five-pound bag of flour. She was covered in white powder, and flour pawprints were everywhere. I asked the dog what had happened, and Indy just looked at me with a glance that said, *I cannot imagine what you are referring to.*

Time passed. Our boys grew up and went off to college. I left my job at one college and joined the faculty at another. My mother died at age ninety-four. The mirror, which had reflected a young mom when Indigo first barged through the door, now showed a woman in late middle-age. I had surgery for cataracts. I began to lose my hearing. We all turned gray: me, my spouse, the dogs.

This summer, I took Indigo for one last walk. She was slow and unsteady on her paws. She looked up at me mournfully. *You did say you'd take care of me, when the time came*, her eyes said. *You promised.*

She died on an August afternoon, a tennis ball at her side.

Sometimes, that autumn, I'd find myself looking for her, as if she might be sleeping in one of my children's empty bedrooms. But she wasn't there.

When you lose a dog, you not only lose the animal that has been your friend, you also lose a connection to the person you have been. For a dozen years, Indigo had been a constant, part of the glue that held us together. Now she was gone.

Then one day I got a call from the place where we board our dogs when we are out of town. One of their customers was dying of cancer. Her dog, Chloe, was a black Lab, and she needed a home. We rolled our eyes. They had to be kidding. We were in mourning, and we were pretty sure we didn't want another big dog, especially an older one, and we were just too banged up. We told them we were sorry, but no.

Then, one weekend when I picked up Ranger after an overnight stay, I met Chloe. Her face was soft. Maybe I could just take her home for a day? You know how this story ends.

When Chloe entered our house, she was cautious and uncertain. She spent hours that first day going to every corner, sniffing things out. At the end of the day she sat down by the fireplace and gave me a look. *If you wanted*, she seemed to say, *I would stay with you.*

Ranger has a new wingdog.

I had hopes of having a conversation with Chloe's owner, trying to learn what their history had been. I wanted to bring Chloe over to her house so that her owner could know that her dog had a good home, so that the two of them could have a proper farewell. When I finally got through, though, I learned that Chloe's owner had died the week before.

It snowed that night, and I woke up in a room made mysterious by light and stillness. In the morning I sat up and found that Chloe had climbed into bed with us as we slept.

Well? she asked. I touched her soft ears in the bright, quiet room and thought about the gift of grace.

"If you wanted," I said, "I would stay with you, too."

DOTTY

DOTTY, A DOG WHO LIVED AND LOVED

by Suzy Pope

Eighteen months ago, my heart was ripped out. Eighteen months ago, we had to make the decision we dreaded—the decision to allow our beloved dog, Dotty, to be put to sleep. Forever.

I remember that day clearly. Our beautiful girl—the third member of our family, who completed our perfect triangle of love—gone. We would never look into those penetrating eyes, ruffle that extraordinary woolly fur, or hear the funny little mumping noise she made when she wanted something, ever again.

Thirteen years earlier, we had come across a litter of puppies in an unconventional way. My partner, Graham, is a chiropractor. One of his patients, a vet, came to see him. He explained to Graham that he had hurt his back delivering some puppies by Caesarian section. The vet told Graham that the puppies were "mistakes" and needed homes—and that they were lovely. They were also born on my birthday.

The next thing we knew, we were visiting puppies. They lived in a pub with their two doggy parents, who had not been altered. The mum was a black Labrador with a sweet temperament. The dad was a feisty black crossbreed.

I had grown up with dogs and had always wanted a dog of my own, but hadn't really been planning on one at the time. But I knew that as soon as we saw those puppies there would be no going back. Dotty chose us—we never even looked at the others. She fixed us with a stare and wriggled toward us. We collected her three weeks later.

Dotty was naughty. Oh my goodness me, she was naughty. She was fearless too, and willful, and very funny. On the evening of her first birthday, we went out for my birthday meal and left Dotty in her bed in the kitchen. When we returned, she was covered from head to toe in a white, sticky substance. Somehow, she had managed to open a plastic tub of pre-mixed plaster. She then smeared it all over the kitchen floor, and finally . . . she rolled in it. We couldn't wash it off her as it had partially dried, so I spent the next few evenings painstakingly picking the crusty lumps out of her fur while she lay next to me on the sofa without a care in the world.

In the early years I sometimes got frustrated with her. She was a roller. She rolled in disgusting stuff most days. After a while, I could even tell when she was going to do it. Her nose would go up in the air and she would give me a quick look as she calculated just how many seconds she had to get her shoulder down into whatever revolting substance it was before I caught up with her. One time I burst into tears in the middle of a field as she ran circles around me, rolling in cowpat after cowpat until she was absolutely caked in vile-smelling excrement.

We attended training classes for "terrible teenagers." Dotty behaved impeccably in the class, and nobody would believe me when I said she wasn't like that at home. Until she managed to tip over and eat a whole bag of chicken treats belonging to a bulldog named Wendy. We all—Wendy included—watched in disbelief as Dotty inhaled the treats like a vacuum cleaner. I think they believed me then.

She was a champion food thief. Right after she turned one, I brought her to work with me. All staff were given instructions to ensure that all food was out of reach. Nope. Dotty found someone's lunch bag and pulled out some frozen pita bread. Peals of laughter rippled through the office as the owner of the pita bread attempted to pry it out of Dotty's mouth. A tug of war ensued. Dotty won.

Nevertheless, everybody loved her at work. She greeted people as they arrived in the morning, and did her rounds during the day—checking on each person while accepting a stroke behind the ears, or a "buttock rub," which was her preference. She attended many client meetings, some uninvited, and also loved to be involved in interviewing prospective job candidates. One of these candidates arrived for an interview in a fairly short skirt. Dotty took a liking to the moisturizer she was wearing and gave her leg a generous lick. The girl disappeared into the bathroom for twenty minutes, horrified. It turned out she didn't like dogs. She got the job, however, and when she left the company several years later, she told me that she adored Dotty and would miss her very much. Dotty had a way of sneaking into people's hearts, either by making them laugh or by showing them the love and affection they needed.

Dotty had presence. She was a wise, smart dog who made an impression on everyone she met, human or canine. She had a natural authority, and dogs deferred to her even though she never dominated another dog. She didn't need to. They just knew. I think we did too. She was very good at getting what she wanted.

She was great in the car. In her lifetime, I drove over a hundred thousand miles with her—she was my constant companion. On weekends, we'd take her to the beach, and I'd watch the sheer joy on her face as she'd trot into the sea after Graham, and they'd jump waves and swim together. She had such energy and a zest for life.

One time we were walking along, and Dotty was dashing around ahead of us. We thought the beach was empty, but then we heard a shriek. Dotty had stumbled across a couple sharing a romantic picnic and helped herself to their pasta salad. They were very kind about it, fortunately. However, we could never really relax if there was unattended food around.

Another time, Graham took Dotty to some sports fields near our house for a walk, where Graham met a cyclist friend of his. They stopped to chat in the car park, and Graham's friend left his car door open. Ever the dog of stealth, Dotty crept around the car and found an entire packed lunch in the passenger footwell. It was only when she started crunching her way through the crisps that they noticed.

When she was seven, Dotty was diagnosed with cancer. The vet said she'd be lucky to make it to Christmas. We got help via a nontraditional route, and our amazing girl lived for another five years. We managed her cancer, and she lived a full and happy life, until the last few days, when the tumor went bang—as we had known it one day would.

I was home with her when she collapsed in our living room. Her face told me she had no idea what had just happened. I held her, and we lay on the floor together as I thought, *Oh God, this is it. This is the moment I've been dreading*.

We got her to the vet, and she improved slightly. However, there was nothing that would help her, so we brought her home and monitored her closely. She had a quiet few days. She wasn't eating much, and while she could walk, she was wobbly. On that final day, she gave me "the look" and I knew she was saying, *It's time, Mum*. We called the vet, who came to the house within thirty minutes and, after examining her, told us we needed to make a decision.

Graham and I went into the next room for a moment. It seemed wrong to discuss this in front of Dotty. She was such a clever dog; we didn't want her to overhear us. We agreed that we didn't want to see our girl suffer, so we went back into the living room and told the vet our decision. Dotty lay on her mat in my arms, and I gazed into her beautiful eyes one last time as she peacefully slipped away.

Looking at her lifeless body was surreal. I couldn't believe that the amazing life force that was Dotty was no longer there. The vet and her assistant quietly and respectfully gave us a couple of minutes with her, and then they gently lifted her body onto a stretcher and loaded her into the vet ambulance. We decided to have her cremated.

We had been pretty good at holding our emotions together while the vet was there, and we hadn't wanted Dotty to see that we were upset. But as soon as they left with her body, Graham and I looked at each other in disbelief. Our triangle now had only two sides. We cried like we had never cried before.

The next few days and weeks were unbearable. The hole left by Dotty was so vast that it physically hurt. We were bereft, crying at any given moment. I came across Graham sobbing as he cooked the rice for our evening meal. Dotty would always "help him" cook rice. and naturally he would make a little extra, just for her. There were painful reminders everywhere. For me one of these reminders was poached eggs. Dotty would hear the rattle of an egg box from a great distance and like a flash appear by my side. I always poached three eggs—two for me and one for her. After she died, I found I couldn't poach eggs for a long time.

We collected her ashes from the vet a week later. I struggled to see our vibrant, strong girl encapsulated in a tube. I didn't know what to do with them, so I put the beautifully packaged tube next to her toy box in the kitchen. Only I found that I couldn't look at it, and suddenly didn't know what to do with any of her stuff. Her toys, her bed, her bowls, her collar, her lead, her food—everything was a reminder. After a few days, I bravely packed up her things and put them in the loft. I left her bed where it was, however, as I couldn't bring myself to clear it away.

We decided to scatter Dotty's ashes at her favorite beach in Dorset. One Saturday, I picked up the tube, placed it in a small rucksack, and set off for the coast with Graham. Part of me wanted to get it over and done with, but I was also dreading the depth of the emotions it would inevitably release.

We actually had a really great day. We walked along the beach that she had so loved, and when we got to the place where she'd enjoyed her first swim all those years ago, I opened the tube and we let the ashes catch the wind and float away into the sea. It was strangely cathartic, and we felt it was the right thing for us, and for Dotty. She was at peace, and so were we.

We now have the patter of paws in our house and the bed that was Dotty's is again occupied. Flossie is a rescue dog from Cyprus—another beautiful black mixed breed with the all-important sense of fun. She is very loving and has helped us fill the massive void left by Dotty.

We have taken Flossie to the beach in Dorset and showed her where we scattered Dotty's ashes. I think Dotty must have whispered in her ear a few times, because Flossie is full of mischief, too, which suits us perfectly.

There will never be another Dotty, but I am so grateful that she shared her life with us. She is loved and missed by a lot of people, but she gave us so many happy and funny memories that we will treasure always.

And I am delighted to say, that after a short interlude, our little family is once again a triangle of love.

MIRA

MIRA

by Maria Nocik

I was just going to look.

Recently separated, with the new title of "single mom," I was headed to a shelter to see if this adorable mutt I'd seen via email would be a good fit for me and my three-year-old son.

The small shelter looked old and dirty, and with no visible signage I wondered if I was in the right place. When I got out of my car, all I could hear was what sounded like hundreds of dogs in the back of the shelter. The volunteer brought out the scruffy mutt from the email, but I knew right away it was just too hyper for my docile child. She pleaded that I at least look and see if maybe another dog might be a good fit—they had so many dogs that needed homes.

As we walked along the row of kennels in the backyard, a dingo-looking dog walked out of the woods and right over to me, then sat down and stared up. The shelter lady remarked, "Wow. They've been trying to catch that dog for months. They're going to put her down if they catch her."

She had the most beautiful eyes, and I was instantly mesmerized by her sweet face. Without even thinking, I blurted out, "I'll take her!" Everything is a blur when I think about the quick process of adopting her, but I do remember the shelter vet checking her out and saying, "She's good to go!" So I put her in the back of my car, and together we headed home.

It was already getting dark on the drive home, and then it slowly began raining. I kept looking at her in the rearview mirror as she stared up front at me. She didn't bark, whine, or really show much emotion at all—but her tail wagged frequently, so I just smiled and talked to her. I told her about me, my son, and her new life with us. And I questioned my sanity. What was I doing? I got a dog and have nothing—no collar, no leash, no bed, or even food.

A few days passed quickly, and surprisingly, things were going along fine with our new pet. She never really barked, but her emotions always came through in her eyes. I thought how lucky I was to find a good-natured dog who was quiet and gentle, yet protective of our new family, even though I'd known nothing about her when I made the choice to bring her home.

She was the first and only dog I've ever gotten by myself. Because she was a stray, the shelter hadn't named her. The name Mira popped into my head.

About a month later when I let her out early one morning, she scurried back inside quicker than usual and lay down in the laundry room. She'd never really gone there before, but I brought her bed from the living room and put it on the floor.

As I stroked her belly, I felt her abdomen contract and knew something wasn't right. For a brief second, I wondered if she was pregnant—but remembered the shelter vet checking her and thought it couldn't be. As I comforted her, the next thing I knew, she shifted her weight and suddenly a tiny puppy began emerging from her. We looked at each other and then I ran to grab my phone. I called a friend who rehabilitates animals and she told me not to worry, that Mira could do everything herself. My friend did warn me, however, that if a puppy was a breech, I'd have to pull it out. She also told me the process could take several hours and that the placenta would be the last thing she would birth. I didn't go to work that day.

Mira ended up giving birth to a total litter of 6 females and 1 male.

I'd never told my apartment complex that I had a dog, so keeping the puppies till they were old enough was pushing my chances of getting caught. My surrounding new neighbors were very understanding, and the puppies slept a lot—in the beginning. As they grew older they were loud, rambunctious, and their constant care kept me on my toes. Thankfully my job was only ten minutes away, so I'd regularly come home at lunch to herd Mira into my temporary corral in the kitchen to nurse the puppies.

I always wondered what kind of impression I made on my colleagues as I occasionally brought the puppies into the office (in progressively bigger boxes) to pimp their cuteness. I guess my sales tactics paid off, because I was able to find all of them new homes.

As a new single mom, I learned that I could handle many things on my own, and because I was so busy being a caretaker, I didn't have time to be sad about my upcoming divorce. Mira was always there for me; she seemed to sense my emotions and would console me whenever I was sad or upset. She helped me learn to be a strong person on my own.

Mira lived to be ten, and together we had an incredible ride. I used to joke that we were like Thelma and Louise, except that one of us was a canine. She died on Thanksgiving Day, appropriately, since I was so thankful for all the years she had been my best friend.

I believe everything happens for a reason, and I think Mira chose me to help both of us through a difficult time in our lives. I'll never forget the moment she walked up to me and made me look. Oh, and her name? Mira means "look" in Spanish. I'm glad I did.

HARRY

HARRY

by DJ Hill

My friend called to say
she's driving her mother
with her dog Harry
to the animal hospital

She didn't say what ailed the canine
sharing instead her mother's choosing
to pass the time on her cell
making chitchat
with her boyfriend

as poor, miserable Harry
lay languishing on the stiff back seat
hardly raising his head
or mournful eyes
until her mother said to the boyfriend

Couldn't you just talk to Harry?
Hearing your voice might make him feel better.

So the mother, not the friend
cradled the phone close
to the pooch's long, slender ear
and the two listened
as boyfriend crooned

It's okay, boy. You'll be okay.
Good dog. Good boy.

Harry didn't lift his sorrowful
head from the red vinyl seat
His eyes seemed to say to mother, boyfriend, friend—
Good God, it's all come to this.

BAILEY + WEBBER

BAILEY AND WEBBER

by Jason Silverstein

The month my wife and I were married, both my paternal grandparents passed away just weeks apart. It was, as the cliché goes, too much for them to live without each other.

They had been sweethearts at a time when being Jewish in the South required sticking together, taking care of like-minded friends and family, and yet remembering to admire the warmth and beauty of their surroundings. Shirley and Morton were married over fifty years, and while theirs was an imperfect union with the challenges of raising four children, their love was pure and true. An example of sticking together, they were.

Twelve years after they died, as we sat in a cold veterinary office with a clinical nurse, I remembered their example fondly and acutely.

While dogs don't get married, the memory of my grandparents rushed over me. We were saying goodbye to our second dog in three months. After her "sister," Webber, had passed, Bailey's life had become slower, less purposeful, less fun. We recognized the heartbreak. Now, it was her time.

Bailey, a German shorthair pointer, started her adopted/rescued life with us by routinely running ten to twelve miles with either me or my wife, depending on who was training for what race. We had adopted her from a rescue in Texas a couple months after we were married. Quiet and shy at first, the brown-and-white-spotted girl blossomed into what can only be described as a crazy nut with the highest of energy. We were smitten.

Webber, a red-tick coonhound whose once-burnt-orange-colored head had become all white, was less interested in mileage and often displayed the stubbornness of a mule. Webber was born on a farm in Colorado, and the farmer told my parents he was going to shoot the litter if someone didn't take the pups. My mom wouldn't have that, so she saved Webber . . . naming her after the farmer himself in a hint of irony. After a couple years of chasing mountain lions into the brush and running with horses, Webber ultimately became Bailey's sister when my parents sold their farm.

When we drove from Texas to Colorado to pick Webber up, Bailey came along with us. Two very different backgrounds collided that day, and Webber really didn't want much to do with Bailey at first. That soon changed.

The two, over time, became inseparable. They slept together, ate together, played together. They welcomed home our two human daughters and dealt with the fostering of other dogs from time to time. We moved from Dallas to Charlotte with all of our family, and they went from chasing possum and armadillos to running after squirrels and cats. Through many vet visits, travels, laughs, and happier times, they enriched our lives in ways only dogs can do.

And that era was nearing an end.

As we were leaving the vet's office, my oldest daughter turned to her mother and me. Through tears, this innocent child who had youthful career plans turned to us and said, "Daddy, I don't think I want to be a vet anymore."

All we could say, through our own tears, was "You don't have to pick what you want to be when you grow up just yet, honey."

While I loved them both, I admit that Webber's passing had hit me harder than Bailey's did. I'd seen that one coming, but I wasn't ready for her to go. Maybe I'd become numb, but Bailey's death hit all my girls harder, as she had more tolerance for their rambunctious flavor of giving affection.

Less than a day after her declaration of a career choice gone, our oldest started repeating the same phrase enough that my wife—also sensing emptiness in our house—started looking online at rescues.

"I need a dog to hug."

(Tears.)

"I need a dog to hug."

So, despite the still-fresh hurt and care for two dogs who couldn't take care of themselves at the end, we drove to a local rescue. There, we met Finley just a week later. And our home is right again.

CRICKET

MILLION-DOLLAR DOG

by Laura-Lee Pernsky

Cricket is standing on the vet's table, as she has done so many times before, and I watch as the vet palpates her belly. He gently pushes and probes, and I can see the concern on his face. He hasn't said anything, but something is not right—I can feel it in my gut. He then strokes her soft ginger fur and looks at me calmly.

"I feel a mass in her belly, and I think we should do an X-ray."

It is not the first time Cricket has had something wrong with her. We have jokingly called her my million-dollar dog for years, following surgeries for both knees, bladder stones, and the removal of her anal glands. Top it off with special food to combat a chicken allergy, and medication for thyroid issues and arthritis, and you get an idea how the nickname came about. But this time it feels different.

She is only eleven years old, and even though I joke that she needs to live as long as I do, I mean it when I say I am counting on at least sixteen years with her. It is not meant to be.

"I'm afraid she's got a large tumor on her spleen. It's likely attached to the liver as well, and there's nothing we can do but make her comfortable," he explains, handing me a box of tissues.

The tumor was not there in September, but by January it's grown so that it's pressing her stomach, making it difficult for her to eat. The hardest thing to wrap my head around is that a splenic tumor may bleed out suddenly, killing her almost instantly, or it may continue to grow and kill her slowly. Suddenly I'm faced with the knowledge that no matter what decision I make, it ends with me losing my best friend.

Cricket came into my life unexpectedly in 2005. I had just finished my first year of teaching and was enjoying my summer vacation when I met this adorable Pom-Yorkie puppy who resembled a tiny fox with her orange face. At one and a half pounds, she stole my heart as I held her in one hand and she yawned the tiniest of yawns.

When I called home and informed my parents that I'd bought a puppy, my dad was furious. Not that he was wrong—I was just starting out with a busy career ahead of me. Plus, I lived in an apartment and didn't have much money. When he met her three days later, however, it was instant love. That was the beginning of Cricket winning over every person she ever met. I grew so used to hearing people say, "I don't like small dogs, but . . ."

We lived in Ignace, a small town in Northwestern Ontario, for the first four years of her life, and Cricket was something of a celebrity around there. I taught at a K–12 school, and the town had a population of about 1500. A couple of school visits, daily walks around town, and a starring role in my Paris Hilton Halloween costume, and before I knew it, everyone knew Cricket.

The next school where I worked was thirty minutes from my house, so Cricket would come to school with me for the entire day. My class of fourteen grade-six and -seven students quickly learned Cricket's rules. One: Do not pick her up. She loved everyone, but she was always wary of being picked up by anyone other than people she knew best. Two: Let her come to you. Sit down, relax, and you could guarantee that she would make the rounds and come for a visit. One student who struggled with focusing found Cricket particularly therapeutic, and when the day got too overwhelming, he could be found curled up on the cushion with her, stroking her fur and enjoying a moment of peace.

The school I currently work at is considerably larger, so I brought her only on special occasions. Halloween was a favorite, as I would crochet her a costume. Over the years she made an excellent bumblebee, sushi roll, and Minion. At Christmastime, I would put her name in for Secret Santa because the kids always got a kick out of seeing her open her present, which she would do with gusto. At home, this became a bit of a problem, as she would open any gift that smelled remotely interesting. I would often find her wagging tail peeking out from amid the piles of presents at my parents' house.

Aside from winning over the masses with her charm, Cricket was my constant companion. When I struggled with the darkness of depression, she was a constant source of light. When I had to make the difficult decision to end an engagement, she licked away my tears. She made the bad days bearable, the good days even more joyful. How was I supposed to go through the rest of my life without her?

When I took her to the vet a week after we'd found the tumor to see if there was any bleeding, I expressed concern about how to decide when the time was right. The vet assured me that I would know.

I called my parents and invited them up for a day of ice fishing. It was the middle of January, which was usually bitterly cold, but this day was beautiful and mild—Cricket's favorite weather. I strapped her into her sheepskin-lined plaid jacket, and down to the ice we went. It was a perfect day. Dietary concerns for bladder stones and weight management? Out the window. Cricket got more little pieces of bologna out of Grandpa Norm's pockets that day than at any point in her life. It was all about making sure that she ate at all, as the tumor was growing quickly.

The two weeks that followed were bittersweet. Each day was a gift, but one that I would have happily returned if only we could go back to normal. I watched her so closely that I hardly slept, and it was hard not to burst into tears every time I looked at her. I took clippings of fur and made imprints of her paws. I promised myself that once she refused to eat roast beef, that was the sign that our time was up.

It happened, of course, and my boyfriend and I took Monday off work and booked the appointment. If I had had any doubt, the ride to the vet quickly took care of that. As I cradled Cricket gently in my arms, she laid her head down and did not lift it for the entire ride. The dog who used to bound joyfully into the vet's office and run straight to the scale to get weighed couldn't even manage a tail wag for her favorite vet techs—all of whom were there to say goodbye. There wasn't a dry eye in the office, and I held her as the sedative kicked in, feeling her go limp in my arms. When it was over, I held her little face in my hands and kissed her between her closed eyes, and stroked her soft ears one last time. I told her I loved her and left her wrapped in her favorite blanket. The thing that I thought I could never, ever do . . . I did.

What I was not prepared for was the outpouring of condolences from the people Cricket had met over the years. Over a hundred comments on Facebook, as well as conversations, cards, texts, and emails sharing favorite memories and photos, it really hit me that Cricket, the dog of my heart, had touched so many other hearts as well. Past students, family, and friends far and wide took moments out of their day to share in my grief, and each message brought with it fresh tears—but also a deeper love for this tiny dog. And as I perused the messages and gazed at the photographs, I realized that Cricket was not just my million-dollar dog . . . she was priceless.

HAZEL

DOG DISOBEDIENCE

by Mary Trafford

Eight weekly sessions,
you trotted by her side,
listening, watching,
thick strap of leather
collaring your bound energy:
obeying, obeying.

Eighth week. The test.
For good dogs. And you are.
A Good Dog. Today, you'll show her:
all the dogs waiting turn,
good dogs with tense humans,
watching, watching.

Six legs, yours and hers,
keeping pace: Forward ho.
Left turn. About turn. Heel.
Sit. Stay. Good dog. Patpat.
And soon, the final test, the
lo-o-ong sitstay. Wait for it.

Sixty seconds, your test:
to sit, stay; stay still.

You sit, try to stay still.
You shiver, held-in energy
threatens to unleash itself
upon you, waiting, wait.

And you're off! Can't stand it.
Just can't sit still! You're galloping light,
quick, bright, around the other
dogs. They jump-start and they're
off! You, their leader, a cackle of hyenas
wild around the hall, as strained
human voices call:

Come! Stop! Get him! Catch her!
But it's Whee, what fun!
as you run and run and run, as one by one,
each dog is caught and laughter
breathes relief around the hall.
You slow down, you go to her.

She holds you, leans toward you,
and whispers: Good dog.

CHESSIE

CHESSIE

by Melissa Schropp

It was 1996, and my husband, Greg, and I had been in our first house for almost a year. This house came ready for a dog, complete with a fenced yard and a doggie door to the back porch. We'd both been denied dogs growing up. Greg's parents were simply not animal people, so he bonded with neighbors' dogs instead. My mother always told me that we didn't have enough outdoor space for a dog. But the reality was that our house was on a 1.5-acre lot; my mom was simply a cat person and wanted nothing to do with dogs. I eventually stopped asking, and, like Greg, I was also limited to bonding with neighborhood dogs.

But no one could tell us no anymore. We agreed that our ideal dog would be medium-sized, maybe a mix of golden retriever and Lab. When Greg heard about a litter of puppies that were just that mix, free and ready for adoption, it was finally time.

We drove to a rural area outside the city and met all the sweet, wriggly pups. Trying to follow the advice of picking neither the most energetic nor the quietest of the litter, we settled on the little gal who seemed right in the middle and who responded well to us. We brought her home and dived into the unknown territory of dog ownership. Her official name was Chestnut, due to her light tawny-brown color, but she was always just Chessie to us. She was gorgeous, sleek, and smart. We enrolled her in obedience school, and she was consistently the only dog who wouldn't ever quite heel. I never walked her; she walked me. But she mastered most other commands pretty well, and proved to be very clever. Our favorite was having her balance a Milk-Bone biscuit on her nose, perfectly still, until we gave her the OK to flip it up in the air and catch it in her mouth. Chessie was Greg's stalwart mountain-biking companion on many weekend rides, and she was always, *always* up for a good game of fetch, which I believe was her greatest joy in life. She enjoyed her fenced-in yard and porch with the doggie door, and spent most days out back keeping us safe from squirrels and postmen.

I'd had a sweet tuxedo kitty named Pi since before Greg and I got married. She was a mellow girl, but as we soon discovered, she was not unlike my mother with her interest in dogs. Chessie truly adored Pi and spent nine years eagerly trying to win her over. She maintained a respectful distance with her tail thumping joyfully, ready to dodge the sharp-clawed swipe for getting too close. Pi maintained a disdainful superior air for the entirety of their years together. If they could have had a spoken conversation, it would have sounded something like this (imagine Chessie as a Buddy the Elf type):

Chessie: "Oh, yay, gosh, it's YOU! I totally love you! Could I maybe lick you?"

Pi: "Fat chance, loser. Back the F off."

Chessie: "Oh, sure, OK, but hey, I'm super glad you live in my house because you are just THE BEST!"

Repeat. Every. Day.

In the spring of 2005, we were awaiting the imminent birth of our third child, and Pi had reached the ripe old age of sixteen. She began a rather swift and steady decline, and I recognized after just a couple days home from the hospital with our newborn daughter that the situation was untenable, so I made the hard choice to say goodbye to Pi. I took my kindergartner with me to the vet for emotional support (even at six, he was that kind of kid), but I had no intention of bringing Pi's remains home. My son inquired of the vet tech whether we could take her home to bury her. I tried to catch the tech's eye and shake my head no, but failed. My heart sank as the tech replied, "Absolutely, you can do that." I simply couldn't explain to that sweet boy that it would just be easier, in my postpartum fatigue, to let them dispose of her in some mass grave. So after our final goodbyes, we drove around to the back of the office, and they brought out a little casket-shaped cardboard box. We placed it into the back of our minivan and drove home.

"You have to bury the cat," I informed Greg when we got back. "At least four feet deep is what they recommend." Our backyard was still something of a construction zone due to an addition that was being finished, but we managed to find a spot in the back corner under a tulip poplar that would be her final resting place. We had a little memorial marker ready, and my son chose a book to read graveside: *Fred the Cat*, about a beloved cat's funeral. The five of us, including a wriggly toddler and a newborn, gathered around the open grave to pay our last respects.

Chessie sat with us initially, then she wandered off to another part of the yard. She soon returned with one of her favorite toys, which she very deliberately and solemnly dropped into the hole on top of the small cardboard casket. Then she continued to sit quietly with us as we watched Greg fill the hole. That sweet dog paid honor at the very end to the same cat who would never, ever even give her the time of day. Because, loyalty. Pi was part of her pack, after all.

Chessie was with us for another four years after that day. We lost her quite unexpectedly at the age of thirteen, when she went from seemingly fine one morning to awful the same afternoon. Our daughters, while playing out back, reported with great alarm that something was wrong because Chessie wouldn't get up and play with them. We found her crawled up way back underneath some bushes in the far corner of the yard. She was struggling to breathe, foaming at the mouth, and was unable to stand.

We rushed her to the vet while a neighbor watched the kids. "Better say goodbye to her now, just in case," we told the kids, knowing there was a good chance we wouldn't be bringing her back home. And indeed, we did not.

Chessie had been our very first "kid," the beginning of our family. She was there as each one of our three children arrived on the scene. And like many family dogs, she slipped down the hierarchal ladder of importance with each new child—but she handled her demotions with good humor. With five humans at home, there was usually someone around who'd pay her some attention. And even if you couldn't, she just loved you right back anyway.

I think it takes a dog to really show us what unconditional love is. After she passed, we took a several-years-long hiatus from pets before we adopted our current dog, Shadow—an older golden-chow mix whose previous owner could no longer care for him. Shadow is sweet and mellow, but bless his heart, he really can't hold a candle to Chessie; he is as dull as she was clever. I don't think we appreciated how great she was until we had another dog. What I wouldn't give sometimes to be able to toss her a tennis ball again and watch her gracefully leap and twist into the air to catch it, so full of joy for the moment. I also really do hope that somewhere out there, Pi is finally being sweet to her. God knows she earned it.

By the way, we recently added a kitten, Millie, to our family, and she tries her damnedest to get Shadow to be her buddy. But the tables have now turned, and he is willfully oblivious to her.

BATMAN

BATMAN, A DOG STORY

by Kim J. Gifford

I used to think that the perfect dog story would be one where the dog did not die in the end. That would be a wonderful story, but it is not the story of dogs. Their lives are brief—way too brief for our liking. Even those that live to a ripe old age in dog years are here only for a fraction of ours. Little Batman did not live to a ripe old age. He died at five weeks old.

Anyone who raises puppies knows this is not uncommon. Some die during birth, others a few days or weeks later. Some are squished by their mothers or don't emerge from their sacs fast enough. There are so many things that can lead to early canine deaths that you come to accept them as fairly normal. But none of us were willing to accept that Batman could die.

When he was born he looked more bat-like than the other pug puppies—something about the shape of his head and the way his fur stood up on the top. His tiny upright ears sealed the deal—he was Batman. He was the smallest of the litter of six—one of his siblings, a big girl, died at birth, but Batman lived. And he was precocious—the first to open his eyes and the first to walk. But from the beginning he had trouble nursing—continually being pushed out of the way by his bigger brothers and sisters.

My friend Joan, his breeder, helped him out by subsidizing his nursing with goat's milk fed from an eyedropper. And he grew—just not at the rate of his siblings. Then, when he was a couple of weeks old, I was visiting and realized that he was having trouble breathing, and his mother and siblings all but ignored him, as though he was invisible. This was not a good sign. Did his siblings reject him because they knew something was wrong? And just maybe—something was.

Joan separated Batman from the pack and began caring for him 'round the clock. We created a warm bed for him in a sheepskin-lined crate, and occasionally let him out to be with his mom and siblings. Still, his little body seemed to heave in a strange way when he'd breathe. Joan brought him to the vet.

The prognosis wasn't good. The vet did not see any congestion and said that, while it could be an infection of some kind, it was more likely that the little guy's breathing passages were not developing properly and that he was only getting about 20 percent of the air he was breathing. Joan feared she would have to put him down, but because she'd fallen in love with him, she decided to give him a chance to develop.

It wasn't meant to be.

The night he died, I had talked to Joan on the phone. She was on the couch cuddling with Batman, who she said had gotten excited when she'd fed him earlier. Nothing seemed out of the ordinary. "He was so happy to eat his dinner," she said.

Sometime during the night, Joan went to pick Batman up and realized he was gone. This was not the first puppy that had died since I've known Joan, but losing Batman was hard.

For such a little guy with such a very short life, he won the love of many hearts. People loved to hear his story. His bigger, gorgeous siblings almost faded into the background when we spoke of Batman. So much charisma for such a small creature. So much love for such a brief life.

One shouldn't grieve a puppy that shone so brightly. Life is precious, fragile and brief. Love both breaks the heart and gives it shape.

Batman was. He mattered. He only lived five quick weeks, but he charmed us all.

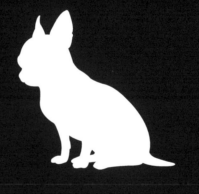

GRIZZLY

GRIZZLY

by Kathy Ingallinera

I wake to the soft colors of the Christmas tree lights shining down on me from a few feet away. I can see Dave sitting at the table drinking coffee, so I know it won't be long before Kathy comes down the hall and starts things in motion with a new pot. I never drink any, but I know that the smell of coffee means a new day.

It's mid-February, and the artificial tree is still up because Dave thinks I like it. And I guess I do like the lights, so colorful and pretty. The tree keeps me company all night long, and I do like company. But the company I like the best is my mom and dad, Kathy and Dave. And right on cue, here she comes down the hall. That means breakfast, but first the kisses and snuggles—my favorite part of each day.

Kathy heads to the kitchen, kisses Dave, and then comes toward me. She slowly gets to her knees, and I lift my head to meet her face with a kiss. She grasps my head in her two hands and gives me several kisses on my nose before I roll onto my left side, ready to receive full-on belly rubs. Both of her hands start to caress my tummy, my chest, my sides and my legs. Ohhhh, it feels so good, especially with all of my lumps and bumps. She scratches my belly and after a while says, "OK, time for breakfast!" and claps her hands together.

As soon as she dishes up my kibble and crumbles a treat into it, I slowly get to my feet and stand for a minute to get my morning legs, then I make my way along the nonskid carpets to my food bowl, where I make quick work of the meal. I turn around and go stand by Kathy so she can give me my peanut butter treats—the ones with pain pills inside them. I get two of those with breakfast, and they are yummy. Once breakfast is over, I go lie down where I can keep an eye on her until she takes me for my morning walk.

When we get back from our walk, I take a nap while Kathy showers. But before she gets in, she squats and says, "You're in for a treat today! Dave and I are taking you to the park for a walk. We have some other surprises too."

I don't always hear everything they say since I am pretty deaf, but I can hear the love in their voices and see the love on their faces, and I know everything is okay. Which is way different from the last place I lived. I put the past out of my mind and start to think about what we're going to do.

Kathy and Dave lift me up into the car. Dave gets in the backseat to help guide me in while Kathy hefts my rear end up, and, somehow, I end up on the seat next to Dave wagging my tail. Off we go!

The first stop is the park. I am so excited, I jump out of the car by myself! Wow, so many new smells and things to see. The trail is a little icy, but I take it in stride. We take a short walk, but it is long enough for me. Back into the car I go after greeting a nice family with kids.

There is still a little snow on the ground, and the air smells fresh and cold. I have the window open a bit so I feel the air rush by my face. It is so wonderful to be out on this pretty day.

We drive along for a little bit until I start to smell food. Kathy pulls into a parking lot and then starts to speak to someone I can't see. Next thing I know, she is handing a bag of food back to Dave and he is unwrapping and then feeding me a Happy Meal! I had a small burger and fries, but Dave drank the vanilla milkshake. My first meal at McDonald's!

We drive a little farther to see the ocean crash on the beach, then turn around and head back toward home. But before that we take a little detour to the raptor center, where they care for injured and sick eagles, owls, and hawks, and where Kathy volunteers every week. I get out of the car and slip on the icy parking lot in my excitement to meet some of the people who work there. As I'm skidding and sliding everywhere, Kathy nearly falls trying to catch me. I get my ice legs, then run up to meet all the ladies for quick kisses before heading back to the car, where I am very grateful for the hoist into the backseat. I am ready for a good nap after such a fun, full day.

As I settle onto my soft, comfy bed under the lights of the Christmas tree, I close my eyes and drift off to sleep, dreaming of pine trees, slippery parking lots, hamburgers, french fries, and the people who love me best of all, Dave and Kathy.

I smile in my sleep, dreaming of the best day ever—and all of the good ones yet to come.

Grizzly passed away on March 3, 2018, after four and a half months with us. He had been abandoned during the summer of 2017 in Sitka, Alaska, where we live on an island in the middle of brown bear country. It was just pure luck that he wasn't killed by one of the bears in the area. The animal control officer picked him up and kept him at the shelter as a mascot, thinking no one would want an old, lumpy, deaf, arthritic black Lab. But we did—and we loved him with everything we had from the moment we met until the day he died.

MAX

MAX

by Jeff Gelberg

It was love at first sight.

We'd known we wanted a German shepherd because we'd already tried one on for size—a rescued puppy named Ruby. She was about five months old and beyond cute. Once we brought her home, she slept on the bed with us. Nipped at our heels. And didn't take to training in the slightest. Then, on the fifth day we had her, in what was probably a bit of overactive puppy play, she decided to jump up and have a quick, light chomp on my daughter's face with her razor puppy teeth. She pierced her skin, drew blood, and scared my daughter.

Only later did we learn that she'd belonged to a homeless man and had lived on the streets since she was born. One day the owner of the rescue had walked by her, recognized Ruby as a purebred German shepherd, and bought her from him.

Poor Ruby had bought herself a one-way ticket back to rescue.

We had learned from the experience that we loved the breed. But we decided that with our next dog, we wanted to know a little more about its history and who the dog was.

The day was sunny and warm when we made the congested drive on the freeway, then halfway up a hill on an unpaved road out to the breeder. They'd just gotten in a litter of German import puppies. We saw pictures of their parents in Germany, knew their bloodline going back five generations.

It was almost too much cute to bear. In one kennel there were five or six playing, all shorthaired shepherds except for this one brutally cute fur ball off to the side. He was quieter and less rambunctious than the rest.

I knew the minute I saw him he was the one.

My wife was drawn more to his sister, one of the shorthairs. But at almost the exact time she was telling me this, the fur ball got up, came over, sat on my wife's feet, and looked up at her.

It's a good thing stealing hearts is legal in California.

We used to joke that Max never read the German shepherd manual. He had no idea how scary or mean he was supposed to be. Not that he was a pushover; he just wasn't a high-strung shepherd, tightly wound and always on alert. He was a sweet guy—unless you were the postman, a stranger coming up our walkway, or someone he didn't like when my daughter was walking him.

I could tell Max to sit, then I'd put a chicken treat halfway in my mouth, lean over, and he'd bare his teeth, get right up to my face and gently take it from me. It scared the hell out of people when I did this in front of them. All I heard was how they'd never let a dog like Max get that close to their face. And sure, I suppose the fear with some German shepherds would be getting your face ripped off. But the thought never crossed my mind. Or his. That's not who he was.

He especially loved to roughhouse in the backyard with my wife, because she was the one who'd really get into it with him. She gave as good as she got, and she was proud of the souvenir bruises up and down her arms that came from their play. When she'd hold his ball before she threw it, he'd jump up and grab her arm with his teeth to try and get it. He'd never bite down; he'd just hold her arm in his mouth like a golden retriever. Maybe it's not so much he didn't read the manual as he read the wrong one.

Max's fighting weight was between eighty-five and ninety-two pounds. He wasn't a small dog, but because we saw him every day, we never thought of him as large—he was just our dog. However, every once in a while, when someone approaching us would suddenly give him a terrified look then cross the street to pass us, or the pizza delivery guy would jump back five feet off my front porch when he saw me holding Max at the door, we'd remember he wasn't exactly a chihuahua.

Max had a lot of nicknames, but my favorite was the one my wife gave him: the Gunslinger. In the middle of the night, he'd come into our bedroom and sleep on the big pillow we had for him on the floor in there. He'd slam our bedroom door open like saloon doors in the old west, then he'd come and crash down on his pillow.

It only gave us heart attacks for the first five or six years.

Almost everyone who came in contact with Max loved him for how beautiful he was inside and out. Because he was a long-haired German shepherd and a lot of people had never seen one before, they loved to tell us he was a mixed breed. We'd just laugh—we knew exactly where he'd come from.

When we got Max, the breeder had stressed how important it was to socialize German shepherds, even more so than most breeds. He was a large dog, and he had to be comfortable around people. So it seemed to me a few bring-your-dog-to-work days was a good place to start.

I was working at a big ad agency when I started socializing Max, and I brought him in a few times to get him used to strangers (believe me, nobody's stranger than people who work in ad agencies). But after people met him, they weren't strangers very long. My coworkers' kindness, caring, and demonstration of love toward Max gave him a sense of confidence and security, and taught him from the beginning people weren't something to be afraid of. I don't know if all of them remember Max, but I'll never forget what they did for him.

Here's another thing: even though Max was the dogliest of dogs, he often seemed to have a cat's nine lives.

Years ago he started to stumble and fall, off balance and confused. At first we were told it was likely Max had a brain tumor. Fortunately, a close friend of ours is one of the premier diagnostic veterinarians in the country. We told David Max's symptoms, sent him the tests, and he diagnosed a bacterial infection. With antibiotics, it cleared up in a few days.

About three years ago, my wife noticed that Max was lethargic and not his usual self. Her Jedi instincts jumped into action, and she rushed him to the vet, where they discovered a giant mass on his spleen, which could have ruptured and killed him at any minute. Again, we turned to David, who arranged for us to bring Max to his practice where there was a surgeon and team standing by at midnight on a Saturday night. At two o'clock in the morning, we got a call: Max had come through his splenectomy just swimmingly.

It was not lost on us how close we'd come to losing him, and we've always considered every day since then gravy.

There was also the time he had his ass kicked by the neighbor's cat and almost got his eyes clawed out, but I'm certain he wouldn't want you to know about that.

In his last few days, he became lethargic in the extreme, not getting up to walk, eat, or pee. We took him to the vet, who saw right away that Max was critically anemic. X-rays revealed a large mass in the cavity where his spleen had been. It was crushing his intestines, and he was bleeding internally either from the mass itself or through it from his liver or kidneys.

There were options, including surgery. But because his red-blood-cell count was so low, he wouldn't survive. Because he was bleeding internally, a transfusion would only have gone into a leaky bucket. None of the options were promising or guaranteed—except to cause him pain, vastly reduce his quality of life, and confuse and scare the hell out of him. He was eleven years old. We weren't going to put him through it.

It's almost always a lose-lose situation when your brain has to win out over your heart.

Since my parents never owned a house, we lived in apartments my whole life, so I could never have dogs growing up. In fact, the house I'm in now is the first one I've ever lived in, and Max was my first dog. Thanks to him, I know I'll never be without a German shepherd.

Max had a very special trick. We didn't train him to do it; he just did it. His trick was making each one of us feel as if he loved us the most (although if I had to place money on it, I'd bet on my daughter). Max will always be the dog of our lives.

So we move on, grateful for having had him as long as we did, and finding peace knowing he's running free in greener pastures. As real dog lovers like to say, he's crossed over the Rainbow Bridge, and he'll be waiting.

It's a crazy world, and the older I get the less sure I am of anything. But there are two things I can say with absolute certainty: Max was well loved every single minute of his beautiful life.

And so were we.

RAISIN

THE YIN-YANG FACE

by Sally Fries

Every night of my childhood ended with me tucking my toes under the warm dog at the foot of the bed. My boxer, Ginger, met my school bus every afternoon, and we were inseparable the rest of the day. We had adventures in the woods, which sometimes ended with her raiding the neighbor's garden and coming home covered in dirt and tomatoes. She would let my sister and me dress her up in costumes. She would knock over grocery bags and devour whatever she could grab. Once it was whole stick of butter. Once a whole bag of chocolate chips—which she later threw up on me. She was as much a part of my upbringing as any friend or relative. We lost her to cancer when I was in high school. With my sister away at college it made for a much too quiet house.

To bond with a dog is to know not only unconditional love but acceptance, empathy, companionship, and pure presence. Somehow, they understand. My husband, John, grew up with Labradors. As young newlyweds we read *Dogs for Dummies*, and after researching every possible breed, I brought John around to the boxer idea. Our research yielded a formula of tests to choose the right puppy, but when I saw the one with the yin-yang face I knew. Raisin's muzzle was black on one side and white on the other. Incidentally, I'm pretty sure she failed all the other criteria. We were smitten and fussed over this puppy like nobody's business. When the babies came and grew to play with her, she was as gentle with them as Ginger had been with me.

At age nine, Raisin got a tumor. The vet wasn't sure whether surgery was an option. I had unexpectedly lost my mother months before and was still treading water in that grief. I told John, "I. Can. Not. Lose. This. Dog. Right. Now." The surgery cost thousands and was miraculously successful. It bought us two more years with Raisin, though her health declined rapidly over the last year. There were lots of medications, a seizure, and the inability to climb the stairs. When she began to lose her appetite, I drove all over town looking for special canned food she might eat. I don't know who was more in denial, the vet or myself. Neither of us was willing to call it.

My boys were young, and they were with me when I drove Raisin to the vet for the final time. Because I was trying to keep it together for them (they had seen enough grieving from me) I was unable to give the vet the necessary orders at that time, but I knew. I had John call the vet later and deliver the instructions.

I did not get the farewell I wanted, or that Raisin deserved. But I did get a two-year reprieve that allowed me to say and do all that needed to be said to and done with my best friend. John was devastated. He said, "They break the bank and then they break your heart." He would later see her in dreams, with her paws up on his lap out on our deck.

We gave away all her things and declared no more dogs.

About a month after her passing, a friend called and said, "Raisin got out." I said, "Raisin's dead." He said, "Well there's a dog that looks just like Raisin taking the nap of its life down the street."

I figured it was a neighbor's dog and walked down the street with a belt since we no longer had a leash. I approached the dog, who was sleeping under a tree. Without looking up he flashed me his emaciated tummy for a rub. Undeniably a speckled boxer belly. And when he did look up, I nearly fell over. A yin-yang face! A friend had said to me after losing her dog that she did not want her next dog to be a replica of the previous one. Here we had a replica, albeit a male with a tail. When John entered the backyard that evening and sat down on the deck, the replica came and put his paws up in his lap.

Seven years later, Wally's yin-yang face is all gray. He is a distinguished senior citizen now and the light of my life. My tween adores him and my teenager frequently Snapchats him to girls. I wouldn't have it any other way. Even knowing how it ends.

TUCKER

JUST A DOG

by Jim Mitchem

When I rolled out of bed Tuesday morning, my wife, Tina, called me into the hallway where she was kneeling next to our thirteen-year-old Australian shepherd, Tucker. "It's time," she said. He appeared to have suffered a stroke during the night. He couldn't control his facial muscles, couldn't see, and couldn't stand. But before I knew any of this, I knew it was time because my wife said it was.

We called the vet and told them we were coming by, and why. Our daughters said tearful farewells and my wife drove them to school. I took my time getting ready that morning. It felt as though my heart was a knotted fist punching down onto my stomach.

Thirteen years earlier, when it was just me and Tina, Tucker went everywhere with us. They knew his name at our beach. He walked the streets of St. Augustine like the mayor. He was a constant companion and positive distraction for us the year my wife worked two jobs to put me through three colleges at once so that I could graduate and we could "get on with our lives." When we moved from Florida to Charlotte, Tucker sat shotgun in the moving truck. When Tina and I bought our first home together, we selected one with a big backyard for dogs and kids. When daughter one was born, her first word was "puppy," in large part due to Tucker's watchful gaze. He was also a good shepherd in raising daughter two. Over the years Tucker helped shape a pack that has seen three other dogs join it. And since we moved, he's been a daily companion for me as I sit at my desk and write.

Thirteen years. They say that's ninety-one in dog years. But it's still thirteen in mine. Thirteen of my possible what, eighty? Probably at least 16 percent of my own life when I'm done. Other than my mother, and now my wife, I haven't been around another soul on this earth on a daily basis as much as I was with Tucker.

Tuesday was hard. Harder than I'd expected. I'd been privy to his sharp physical decline over the past several years, and I had tried to prepare myself for the day we'd eventually have to put him down. My wife kept hoping for a *My Dog Skip* ending, but I was convinced that his body would break before his spirit. He had been on anti-inflammatory medications for three years. He'd lost his hearing. I had to carry him down the back steps at night. Our measuring stick had become whether he was still smiling or not. But he did. He always did. Right up to the morning of his death.

Instead of going directly to the vet, I drove to the park one last time. It wasn't an attempt to see whether he was getting any better, or to delay the inevitable, it was just me and him spending a few minutes alone together like we had so often for so many years. I carried him out into the field and placed him down. He collapsed. I stood him up, holding his rear legs, but he couldn't find his balance and collapsed again. Despite this, he frustratingly tried to stand using only his front legs. That's not how I wanted to remember his last few moments, so I carried him back to the truck and set him on the rear seat. Then, as his blind eyes caught me standing in front of him, he smiled. And at that moment, I knew that he knew it was time too.

On the way to the vet, I stopped and picked up a king-size Butterfinger, then sat sobbing in the vet's parking lot until my wife arrived. They placed a blanket on the floor of an examining room, and that's where we said our goodbyes. I held him tightly and rubbed his ears as they placed the catheter into his vein. The doctor left us alone for a while longer. We kissed and hugged him and washed him with our tears. Then we gathered our strength as the doctor returned. Before she inserted the needle, I pulled out the Butterfinger. The way I figured it, God played a trick on dogs by making it deadly for them to eat chocolate. Letting Tucker indulge at this point was my way of getting God back for playing His trick on people—giving dogs such short lives.

As the vet pressed down on the plunger of the syringe, I wrapped my arms under his chest, pressed my face against his ear, and whispered, "Everything is going to be all right." Then I shut my eyes tight and waited. His breathing slowed, and a moment later, his body went limp in my arms. And my loyal friend for so many years was gone. But at peace.

MARLEE

A LIFETIME JUST YESTERDAY

by Lindsay Oakley

It's been nearly a month since I said goodbye to you, Marlee, and it feels like it was just yesterday.

Just yesterday, I was waking up to your cold nose in my face and the sound of your tail thumping against the bed when you saw me open my eyes. Just yesterday, I was listening to your happy "wooooo-woooooo" when greeting a family member or anticipating food. Just yesterday, that doggy grin with that lolling tongue was making me laugh.

It was only yesterday I found out how much we trusted each other, how much we relied on each other, how far you'd come with your training, and what a great team we made.

It was yesterday, I swear, that we discovered how good you were at trimming your own nails. How much stress was relieved when you realized I wouldn't push you past your comfort zone, so you went even further than I thought possible.

And wasn't it just yesterday that you got your champion-trick-dog title? You certainly were a little smarty pants, picking up tricks faster than any dog I'd ever seen.

Yesterday, I was helping you build up your toy drive. We played Frisbee, and your eyes would just get huge every time I'd say "Go around." You were pretty good at catching, no matter how lousy my throws were.

Right around yesterday, we found trails you loved to run on, trails where it was only you and me, where you ran and ran without worrying about anything.

Seems like just yesterday that I noticed a tiny lump on your neck and took you to the vet.

Yesterday, your right pupil turned red, you had a hard time seeing, you couldn't bend, you couldn't get comfortable, and walking required my help.

Only yesterday, my heart shattered into so many little pieces that even when put back together, still didn't fit right—and left a gaping hole.

Yesterday, I held you for the last time, and said the hardest goodbye I've ever had to say.

Just yesterday, I got you back in a little box, a shell of what you once were. A constant reminder of the indelible impression your tiny paws left on my heart.

Tomorrow, I'll keep going. But for right now, at least, I'm living in a lifetime of yesterdays.

LELLU

THE GOOD DOG

by Elizabeth Swann

Hushpuppy. Mocha. Biscuit. Not sure why, but most of my dogs end up with names that also happen to be food. I'm sure they'd approve.

One who wasn't named for something tasty was Lellu, an insatiable yellow lab. Lellu earned her moniker from my four-year-old son, Andrew, who couldn't pronounce the word *yellow*. He said, "Lellu." And so she was.

As a puppy, Lellu was a chewer. From chairs to shoes to the base molding in the kitchen—you name it. There was a while there when we were sure Lellu was part piranha.

By the time she was seven months old, it was clear she needed a trainer. She'd lost her needle teeth, but because she was so cute, she got away with too much. And she'd eat anything—citronella candles, plastic garden sprinklers, the house, the list goes on. So we hired Larry.

Larry is a Carolina guy with a two-ton Southern accent and an even bigger heart. He's got a place in the country with one house for himself and his wife, and one house to train dogs. The dog house is the newer, bigger house. His home office is covered with wall-to-wall photos of his dogs—the ones he trains and boards.

Of course, he has his own canine, too—a sleek German shepherd named Schindler. And Schindler helps him train the other dogs because . . . he's perfect. Unlike my little Lellu, the happy-go-lucky piranha woodchipper. Remarkably, Larry straightened out Lellu in no time. Which is to say, he straightened *us* out in no time. Dog training, I learned, is more about training the owners than the dogs. And consistency is key. So I trained. Unfortunately, my husband (aka "the Marshmallow") was less trainable. He is a sucker for puppy-dog eyes, but I am a high school teacher and am made of sterner stuff. It wasn't long before Lellu knew who was boss, and as a result she became less of a voracious lion and more of a snuggly lamb. It was brilliant.

After that we took her everywhere, and with the words "car ride," she would make a vertical leap that could rival Michael Jordan's into the back of the station wagon.

But then, at only ten months, Lellu stopped leaping. Excited for the car ride, tail wagging, she'd get out to the car—and sit.

"Up, up! Let's go, Lellu! Car ride!" I would say. But she just sat and looked up at me until I lifted her into the car.

A trip to the vet confirmed my suspicion that she had terrible hip dysplasia. Bad genes. Bad luck. Bad breeder. It was all bad news.

With blurry, tear-filled eyes, I took the bottle of pills home with my sweet pup. Under doc's orders, I kept her inside a lot and carried her up and down the steps to go out. She was hurting, and the vet warned us that it might take a while for the medicine to work.

Surgery cost thousands, so meds would be the first line of defense. It was heartbreaking—Lellu was still a puppy.

By now it was fall, and the leaves were turning scarlet and umber, but they hadn't yet fallen. Still holding on. Just like Lellu.

After a few weeks, Lellu could go out more, and she generally went right to her new spot, a snuggly place in the ivy on the far side of the driveway. Andrew spent more time at preschool during this time, but he always looked forward to coming home to a wagging tail and sloppy kisses.

One day, as I was running a little late for a school function, I decided to leave Lellu out in the yard. She always just stayed in her spot now, and she had been well trained on the invisible fence. I wouldn't be gone long. I watched her in the rearview mirror as I backed out of the garage. There she was in her spot, lifting her head as if to say goodbye. Near the end of the driveway, there was a collision.

No. Please God, no.

I threw the car into park and ran to the back of the station wagon.

It was Lellu.

It was bad.

She must've struggled to get up to trot alongside the car near the edge of our yard until she ran out of room and hit the invisible fence. And, like a good dog, she ran away from the fence—and under my car.

She was on her side, and there was blood. We were both crying. I rushed to pick her up to put her in the back of the station wagon. She bit my hand. She was in shock. I somehow got her into the car and raced to the vet's office. I ran inside—but I couldn't speak. I just held out my trembling, bloody hands.

A vet tech cried out, "Cat or dog?"

"Dog," I choked out.

And they went into action. I don't remember what happened next, but somebody gave me a cup of water. And a blanket. And they must've cleaned me up and bandaged my hand.

Then I remembered—Andrew. But they wouldn't let me leave the vet. I was in shock too.

Sometime later, the vet emerged from the back. He shook his head. Broken forelegs, internal bleeding. I don't even remember what all. I don't want to remember.

They figured she'd suffered enough, and recovery on top of the hip dysplasia would be next to impossible. They recommended putting her down. But it was our decision.

I couldn't do it. Not yet. I had to get my son. I had to call my husband.

In the end, I went back, alone, while my family ate dinner. I wasn't hungry. I sat with Lellu while the vet filled a syringe and injected the pentobarbital into the IV. Then he left us, and I stroked her silky ears. Her downy forehead. "Good girl. Good girl. You're such a good girl, Lellu."

Then I saw the light leave her eyes. I'd never experienced death before, but that's exactly what it was like. The light just faded away. It was Lellu—and then it wasn't anymore. She was gone.

I sobbed. How could I have been so careless? So stupid?

It took some time, but I got myself together as best I could. I went home clutching her blue collar to my chest.

I had to tell Andrew something, so I explained that Lellu had been hit by a car. I've never told him who was driving.

In the days that followed I cried a lot. In fact, I cried while writing this confession—which was written many years after Lellu's tragic loss. But when the tears did flow just now, Biscuit came swaggering in and plopped his big wet nose in my lap. He was Lellu's replacement—as if any dog (or any person) can replace another. He and Lellu are totally different. Biscuit is a goofy people-pleaser who never touched a shoe or chewed on anything that wasn't his. Yes, Larry trained me well. Now Biscuit is thirteen years old.

Deep down, I have to admit, I love a rebel girl who wants to gobble up the entire world and take it all in. So yeah, I still have the chewed chair with the rough, splintery teeth marks on the stretchers where Lellu gnawed while she was teething.

And I'm keeping it. She was a good dog.

ROCKY

ROCKY

by Darren Maurer

Dearest Rocky,

Just moments ago, I watched you sail, catlike, into the air while grabbing a ball that had bounced awry. I'm befuddled that you remain so athletic despite the cancer reaching its hideous tentacles throughout your hips. Your pain tolerance is remarkable, and it cleverly masked the aggressive disease that's been growing inside of you. Tomorrow I will hold you for our final goodbye.

You entered my life as a working police dog that wasn't "good enough" to stay in the Netherlands. You showcased extreme focus and intensity right from the start—traits that later elevated you to greatness. On the training field you moved with grace, nearly floating at times. On the street, you put forth Herculean efforts and accomplished things few other police K9s ever will. You ranked high in work ethic and fearless intensity. You were among the best with unnerving confidence and calmness in the throes of chaos.

I marveled in awe when you were shot. Shot, but still able to chase and apprehend the shooter. Tears were shed not only for the pain you endured while healing, but also for the heroic effort you put forth that night. That night you passed the ultimate test that training cannot replicate, one very few creatures on this earth could pass. It was fitting that the American Police Hall of Fame and Museum somehow heard about your story and recognized you. Valor Awards from national K9 organizations as well as from the Kong Company added to your legacy.

There are other work stories, too. The fugitive hiding underwater that you literally swam above until he eventually came up for air and you grabbed him. The armed robbery suspect hiding under a trailer that you extracted via his head. The car thieves, the burglars, the sex-assault suspect, the reportedly armed and dangerous man you found lying in a creek . . . the list goes on and on. Yes, we missed some, but you found your share, and I rode on your coattails.

Three years after being shot, you competed with thirty-eight other K9 teams from across the state, and you stoically trotted off the field with the championship trophy. The following year I screwed up a repeat performance, but you still won several individual event trophies. People who knew you respected you. Even the fugitive that you bit in the face later remarked that you were "a great dog!" I cherish that comment, proof that you valiantly earned respect even from those you hunted. Steadily, I just followed you, nearly bursting with pride that you were my K9. My partner. My companion. My protector. My best friend.

August 4 will no doubt forever be etched as a monumental date in my life: your last day falls on the anniversary of the day you were shot.

I'm grateful that you were able to enjoy nineteen months of retirement, and how I wish you still had years left to share with the family. You have been a pleasure at home. While I commonly referred to you as Dr. Jekyll and Mr. Hyde due to your transformation when it was time to work, you were always balanced enough to know that home was a place of rest, play, relaxation, peace, and love.

Oh, the things I will miss. Your sparring with the lawn sprinkler. The stallion-like prancing along the fence at bicyclists riding past. That lip-fluttering long exhale when you lie down at home, as if blowing out the day's efforts. That drawn-out groan that trails off as you drift into sleep. Those long, deep breaths of contented slumber. The puppy-like whimpers accompanying twitching feet that always make me smile as I imagine you dreaming about chasing balls, decoys, or bad guys. I'll miss that big wet nose bumping me awake and that rarely seen wagging tail that wonderfully greeted me in the mornings. Not having those "good mornings" from you will make me not want to wake. Instead, after tomorrow, I will awaken and look for you. It will take a lot of time for me to register that you're gone. The mere thought of this makes my chest hurt.

Rocky, I've dreaded this end for many years. A few close friends have heard me talk about this inevitable day. I had hoped talking about it in advance would help me cope, but I fear, actually I now know, I will be an absolute mess when you're gone.

What will I do? No Rocky in my life seems like fiction. We were a team, and I am grateful and truly blessed that our paths crossed. You brought so many things to me, both at work and at home, and I honor and salute you.

It's been said that the dog becomes like his master. I cannot, and will not, accept credit in "forming" you. You became great because that's just who you always were. I was simply the person who inserted you into some tough situations that allowed you to do what you were born to do.

I don't want to stop writing because finishing this letter means I'm that much closer to saying goodbye. I was hoping for several more years together and my hopes have been dashed. I am crushed.

I originally thought I would wait outside while the vet administered the medicine that would allow you to sleep forever, but that's not the way it should be. We were always at our best side by side. My face will be your last vision and my voice will be the last sound you hear.

I hope I upheld my end of the bargain by providing the life you wanted, because you definitely exceeded your end of it.

Thank you, Rocky. You greatly enriched my life in so many facets. I will painfully miss you.

I love you.
Darren

MAX + KAYLA

BARON MAXIMUS OF PETNIC

by Yolande du Preez

My mother passed away on October 12, 2009, after a short but cruel battle with cancer. She died at her home in a retirement village after being in a semiconscious state for five days. She was only sixty-four years old.

As an only child, my mother's illness consumed my time. I was married, and although my husband was very supportive, I felt it was my duty as my mother's only daughter to care for her. Working, furthering my studies, and looking after my family was not easy—but I wanted to do it. Needed to do it.

During my mother's final days, as I lived next to her bed and as struggled to say goodbye, my Scottish terrier of eight years, Max, was fighting his own battle.

I grew up with animals who were treated like children. They slept on the bed and ate from the table. Nothing was taboo for them, and nothing much has changed since. We are animal lovers. I have always loved Scottish terriers. The regal look combined with stubby little legs, pointy alert ears, and a skirt. I say it's the only breed that can rock a beard and a skirt at the same time.

My husband and I bought Max in 2002, soon after we were married. He was not registered with the Kennel Union of Southern Africa (KUSA), and at the time we hadn't done much research on the breed. He was a Scottie, and that was all that mattered. He was everything I expected, and I adored his stubby legs. He was the apple of his mama's eye.

Six weeks after we got Max, we decided to get him a partner in crime and started looking for puppies in our area.

This time we came across a breeder, and Max's "sister," Kayla, was KUSA registered. Her name was Baroness Mikayla of Kananna, and to make sure Max didn't feel neglected, we decided to give him a posh name, too, and so he became Baron Maximus of Petnic. Max and Kayla for short.

Eight weeks before my mother died, Max was having difficulty eating. Our vet discovered an abscessed tooth, so he pulled the tooth and prescribed some antibiotics. A week after the tooth extraction, however, Max was still not himself, so we made another trip to the vet. This time the vet took a blood sample. That's when were told that Max was suffering from autoimmune disease. He was prescribed cortisone tablets and more antibiotics. But before he could finish the scheduled dosage of cortisone, his health deteriorated, he lost his appetite, and he became anemically lethargic, sleeping throughout the day. This time our vet had no answers, and instead referred us to University of Pretoria Faculty of Veterinary Science. The first appointment we could get was a week later. Max's health improved that week to the point where he regained his appetite.

The same could not be said for my mother. She'd lost consciousness, and we were told by hospice staff that it would not be long. Since Max was doing better, we rescheduled his appointment so that I could focus all my attention on my mother.

The hours next to her bed became a blur, and one day I realized I hadn't been home in three days. My husband would fetch me fresh clothes and tended to things at home. On the afternoon of October 12, he convinced me to leave my mother's side to grab a bite to eat and refresh my perspective. I reluctantly agreed, and as we arrived at the mall, I received the call I was dreading. My mother had died. And I was not by her side during her last moments.

The next morning I had three appointments. One with the dentist, one with the funeral parlor, and one at the university for Max. I decided to go to the dentist. I wanted to do something normal.

I remember how I thought to myself on the way back that we should not take too long at the funeral parlor as we could not be late for Max's appointment. As I turned into our driveway, my phone rang.

It was my husband. "Come quickly. Something is wrong with Max," he said.

I jumped out of my car and ran into the house. Max was on his side, convulsing, and my husband was giving him mouth-to-mouth.

We put him on a towel and carried him to the car while my husband was still doing CPR, saying, "Come on, Max, come on, boy."

I thought if we could just keep him alive long enough to get to the vet, he would be OK.

We didn't make it out of the driveway.

An autopsy revealed that Max, too, had died from cancer.

Max decided to go with my mother—but he'd waited for me.

SYDNEY

HUGE LITTLE DOG

by Russ Dymond

Dear American Kennel Club:

I am aware of your classification of dogs into different groups—Sporting, Hound, Working, Terrier, Toy, Non-Sporting, Herding—and one other murky group called Miscellaneous, apparently made up of breeds that haven't quite made the grade into any of the other groups but someday might. I am sure these classifications serve useful purposes, but I have personal knowledge that they do not catalog all dogs properly. As such, I am writing to advocate on behalf of an additional group, which would be called the Huge Group. A prime candidate for this group is a breed that is completely misplaced in its current group: the Australian terrier.

According to your organization's information about this breed, adult Australian terriers, or Aussies, as they are called, are ideally ten to eleven inches tall and weigh twelve to fourteen pounds. This would make the Aussie a small dog, but I can tell you from experience that these statistics don't begin to measure my Aussie. She was no small dog.

I got Sydney as an eight-week-old puppy from an AKC breeder. The breeder, who was from out of town, personally delivered her to my office. She was little then, about four to five inches tall and less than a foot long. After holding her in my arms, I placed her on the floor. She looked up at me, which must have been like looking up at a giant, and promptly peed. From that moment she started growing. And she became a giant.

Sydney was variously described as being blue and tan or blue and red. Neither was correct. Her head and shoulders were like spun gold. The top of her head was crowned with a small tassel that arched forward. She had a small, black nose, and behind it, a sculpted, flat muzzle. Her dark, clear eyes were ringed with black, a gift of permanent mascara perfectly applied by Mother Nature. She was beautiful, and almost everywhere we went together, people would stop me and ask about her—her name, her breed, and where could they get a dog just like Sydney.

The fact was, they couldn't. Even if they were fortunate enough to acquire an Aussie, it wouldn't be like Sydney. Sydney was unique.

She was also lightning fast, fearless, and a born leader. I cannot tell you how many times people stopped me, leash in hand with Sydney twenty feet in front of me tugging away, and asked, "Are you walking her or is she walking you?"

"Laid-back," you see, was not part of Sydney's DNA. The sound of dog food hitting her bowl caused a pogo-stick reaction, and spinning in wild circles. The sight of her leash in the morning would send her running from room to room in joyous anticipation. And any opportunity to leap would find her in midair. She would leap over puddles, cracks in sidewalks, manhole covers, curbs. It didn't matter. What mattered was high octane.

Perhaps it was because Sydney was so full of life that the importance of quiet times with her was magnified. I liked to rub her soft belly, to stroke her head, to hold her paw, to see her lick my hand or feel her lick my face. I loved to see her senses at work and how she interpreted the world: snow was a wonder; ice, a mystery; thunder, a menace; ocean waves, a game.

Life, in fact, was a game to Sydney. She liked to play keep-away with a rubber ball, hide-and-seek; and top this, wherein I would put my foot lightly on top of her paw and she would put her other paw on top of mine, and so on. She loved it when I pretended to stalk her. And sometimes, I'd come inside out of the sun with my baseball hat on, then take it off and say, "Hey, Syd! Wanna wear my hat?" and she would put her little head down and walk to me. I'd put the hat on her head backward and say, "Syd! You look great in my hat," at which time she would invariably shake it off. Sydney kept me laughing.

And she became part of my identity. In the same way people would ask about a wife or a loved one, "How's Sydney?" was the question they asked me. Her care affected everything I did. My mornings because I needed to feed her and take her out. My evenings because I needed to get home at a decent hour to repeat what I had done in the morning. My weekends and vacations because I had to plan for her care.

In return, the care I received from Sydney was automatic and immense. She helped me get through the death of my mother, the death of my brother, and the death of my IRA. She turned bad days at the office into good evenings at home. She taught me what it was like to view each day as a new beginning. Each meal an event. Each walk an adventure. Each person we met on the way a potential new friend.

Sydney was no small dog. She was bigger than life.

But, ironically, life was not kind to her.

At a very young age, she began to have seizures that would cause her to black out and fall. Worse than this were recurring blockages in her urinary tract that caused her to pass blood. She never seemed to be in any pain, but it was obviously a serious condition, and I tried everything I could to find the cause and correct it: blood tests, X-rays, drugs, prescription food. Nothing worked. Then, when she was twelve, she became partially deaf. About that same time, she was diagnosed with Cushing's disease, and before the vet got it under control, she almost died. But it was the blockages that were so terrible. Each one required surgery. While recovering from her third operation, one month and four days before her fourteenth birthday, she suffered a stroke and died.

I still wake at the same time Sydney always barked for me to get up. I automatically sit on one side of the big den chair we shared every morning after breakfast. I habitually look for her before pushing back the chair from my desk. At three o'clock, I think we should be going for a walk. In time, I suppose, these habits will lessen and finally disappear. The memory of Sydney, however, will not.

For almost fourteen years, Sydney was the overwhelming presence in my life. Her loss has been immeasurable. And so, American Kennel Club, you need to add another category—another group for Australian terriers. You need to elevate them to the Huge Group. Because Sydney was no small dog. If she were, how could losing her leave such an enormous hole in my heart?

Respectfully,
Russell L. Dymond

JOSIE

YOU NEVER KNOW

by Pam Desloges

Sometimes you never get to see the far-reaching impact of your deeds. But then again, sometimes you do.

When Josie and I picked each other out at the animal shelter, I whispered in her ear that we would have good times, and her eyes sparkled in reply. We hiked mountains, canoed lakes, sat on the village green during summer concerts, spent long weekends with friends in Maine, took walks in snowstorms while waiting for the plow to clear our driveway. She traveled with me from Maine to Alaska and down to Florida. She was seldom on a leash and was welcome everywhere. I always felt safer traveling with her, although she couldn't drive a standard or read a map.

Josie was a border collie/Lab mix who had a subtle but profound effect on people. When we had been together for two years, I decided it was time for her to get a job. She had earned her Canine Good Citizen Certificate at a local dog show after I signed her up on a whim; she would be perfect for therapy-dog work.

Near our house in the mountains of New Hampshire, there was a private nursing home called The Log Cabin. It actually had log siding and sat off the road in a forested area. It was small—with maybe twenty to twenty-five residents. I brought Josie to meet the director, who reviewed our credentials and was delighted at the idea of my bringing Josie to visit the residents every week. Soon we were spending our Wednesday mornings there.

I initially consulted with the staff about which rooms to enter, and always asked each resident if they would like to see the dog. Some declined. Most, however, were glad to have us visit them. We spent about fifteen minutes in each room, with lots of laughter and chatting. We enjoyed our visits and getting to know the folks.

I remember Alice, who chirped with delight when she saw Josie. Every week, she rubbed Josie's head and crooned, "What a sweet dog! What's her name?"

"Josie."

"How old is she?"

"She's four."

"I had dogs. I always had dogs. Big ones like this. What's her name?"

"Josie."

"How old is she?"

Alice was one of our favorites.

On the second floor, there were fewer rooms; the people there seemed more independent. I guessed that they might have been there because they had no other place to live.

The first time we knocked on the open door of room 206, a woman answered that she did not care for a visit from a dog, but would love to chat with me for a few minutes anyway. Josie and I went in, and Dorothy offered me a chair next to her rocker. While we talked, Josie lay quietly on the floor beside me, pretty much unnoticed. Dorothy was physically fit, mentally alert, and interesting to talk with. I enjoyed our short conversations. Dorothy had a niece who lived nearby and came every week to take her out to lunch and make sure she had everything she needed.

One Wednesday, I looked into Dorothy's room and she wasn't there. I assumed she was out with her niece and proceeded down the hallway.

The next week when Josie and I got to her door, I was relieved to see her sitting in her rocking chair. As soon as she saw us, she called out for us to come in. "Bring the dog over here." She reached out and ran her thin fingers over Josie's smooth fur. During our visit, she never took her hands off Josie and gazed at her constantly.

She explained that the previous week, she had experienced a "heart incident." Emergency personnel were summoned and whisked her to the hospital. She said that the ambulance ride was overwhelming, and she was terrified that she was going to die.

"But then I thought of your dog. I kept envisioning her and that comforted me. I pictured her while I was in the emergency room. She was with me all the time at the hospital." Dorothy held Josie's face in her hands and kissed her on the nose. "I don't think I could have made it without her."

Josie and I spent fifteen years together until she died of old age. Now I, too, picture her. When I think of her, my skin hurts because I miss her so much. But, like Dorothy, I feel a great calm when I see her face. I, too, think of many times that I could not have made it without her.

Sometimes you never know. But I always knew. Right from the moment I clipped a leash onto her collar at the animal shelter. When her soft golden eyes looked into mine and said, *We're good*.

We were. Together, we were the best.

TRAJAN

BECAUSE THAT'S WHAT YOU DO

by Melissa Culbertson

He stepped his little yellow paws into the cold, clean water that filled his brand-new stainless bowl. And stared.

At us. His new owners. Two not-quite-newlywed-but-still-young Carolina kids over two thousand miles away from home settling into a new life in Arizona. Two kids who moved across the country with a taste of adventure on their tongues.

A month later, those two kids had fresh new jobs, so we took the next logical step any young married couple would do: we got a puppy. We named him Trajan after a roman emperor with architectural ties. Given my graphic design background, I loved the idea that the name was also a font. So it stuck.

We spent hours training him. Teaching him to paw a bell when he wanted to go out. Sit. Shake. Whisper. Bow. Roll over. Play dead.

We took him on adventures big and small. Making fast friends at the dog park. Trotting through long, sometimes steep hikes. Chilling at camp sites with his dog buddies. He even saw the Grand Canyon.

And boy did he love to swim. Most people in Arizona have pools, so he took any possible opportunity to jump in and swim swim swim. God made Labradors for that.

Fast-forward thirteen and a half years. We're now two newly-forty adults living back in the Carolinas (just the north one this time). Except we now have kids of our own. Their childhood came with a dog: the default setting, an ever-present part of growing up. They know no other way.

Our kids don't really remember much of the energetic, adventurous Trajan. As the kids grew to form memories that stay tucked in their minds, there were only glimpses of that version of our dog. And there were definitely no traces of the unsure little pup that sat in my lap on the car ride to his forever home. He was cozy and comfortable with his life, even if his body eventually wasn't.

He had a host of health issues that would rival any old man: diabetes for eight years, blindness for six, one "dead" eye for three, Cushing's disease for a few years, deafness for around eighteen months, and so on. Yet he was resilient in every way possible.

He hadn't slept through the night with any regularity for a few years. And neither had we. Instead, we'd sleepily shuffle from the downstairs master bedroom to the back door to let him out in the middle of the night. Multiple times a night. Because that's what pet owners do. What we need to do. We adapt, even if it's inconvenient.

And when he started losing control of his legs a few months ago, we'd reach underneath him and boost his body up so he could walk to his destination. Sometimes twenty times a day. Because that's what you do.

And when he started losing control of his bowels without realizing what had happened, we'd just grab some toilet paper and clean it up. Because that's what you do.

Years ago, upon learning Trajan was going blind, I remember a vet telling us "you should consider not keeping him since you have young children at home." We never spoke to her again. It never even crossed our minds that he wouldn't be with us until the end, no matter his conditions. Because when your dog is family, that's what you do.

We gave him almost six thousand injections over the years. Probably two hundred doses of his weekly chemo pills for Cushing's. And who knows how much other medicine. We would have kept it up. But he was ready to let go.

Trajan, the Lab who used to run laps around the backyard, full of excitement. Trajan, who left a bare spot in the grass because he loved to roll in that exact spot. Trajan, who'd perch his muzzle at the edge of the couch, hoping for some buttery popcorn. Trajan, the wonder Lab who went on so many adventures. Trajan, who was weary.

When I made the call to our vet to discuss his worsening health, I told him that I guessed I was waiting for an "event" that would make the choice easy for us. And our vet, knowing Trajan so well, said, "Trajan is a fighter. He just rolls with the punches, so I don't know that you'll get that from him." He was right.

The truth was that Trajan had been giving us "events" for months. Like tremors that come before an earthquake. The nighttime roaming, the panting, the back legs not working, the days I'd come home from work to find him lying on the floor because he couldn't get up. Independently, these scenarios were easier to accept, but when we started to connect the dots, we saw the bigger picture of his health. And it wasn't good.

Deep breaths, I told myself. It will be okay. He will be free of his limiting body.

I picked up the phone and made the appointment. After I hung up, my husband and I held each other on the back porch and sobbed.

Emperor Trajan of Arizona was put to sleep on a Tuesday. He was three months shy of fourteen years.

A few days before, we'd told the kids the news. All four of us sat on a couch and bawled. The kids had never seen their dad cry before. The staggering news paired with the evidence of their parents' pain showed in their eyes. I'll never forget that.

The next few days were filled with lots of Trajan time and treat giving. His last dinner was a Five Guys burger. I sat on the floor with him and shared a bowl of popcorn. He got one last walk with just my husband and me, sniffing all there was to sniff. Then we hoisted him into the car for one last ride, with the windows down so he could feel the spring breeze on his face. He couldn't see, and he couldn't hear, but feel he could. And he did. The experience was heart-wrenching, but I couldn't imagine not being there for him.

It started with us. Picking up a yellow, floppy-pawed pup who would change our lives. It ended with us. Stroking the body of a soft-eared, hazy-eyed dog as his final moment slipped away.

We puddled on the floor beside him, crying over the body that remained. Trajan, however, had moved on. He softly passed to a world where he's running free with eyes that can see, ears that can hear, and legs that don't give out.

A piece of me floated away with him that day. When I looked at Trajan, I saw an old pup who lived a long, happy life. I saw my life reflected. A life when it was just two young souls with an adventurous dog. A life with children running through the house and a loyal dog by their side. Me going through my twenties, thirties, and turning the corner of forty. From prancing puppy to unsteady old dog, I witnessed the full life of God's creature within a sliver of my own. He embodied a piece of time. And that time was now gone.

Parts of Trajan still linger around the house. A ball of fur in the corner. A bone under the couch. A dog bed with his imprints still visible. We have his ashes in an unadorned mahogany box. And a beautiful portrait of him my sister painted. He's with us, even if I don't hear the clicking of his paws traipsing across the hardwoods any longer.

Sometimes I cry because he's gone, and sometimes I still walk through the door thinking he'll be lying on our bedroom floor.

Loss screams in your face, then is faint like a whisper. And back and forth and back and forth. But faith reminds you that it'll all be okay.

It'll be okay.

ACKNOWLEDGMENTS

What began in 2014 after the death of a family dog is now the book you hold in your hands. It's been a long road filled with learning experiences and tons of new people. (And new dogs.) We're proud of our work and want to thank the people who helped make it possible.

To our fans who helped spread the word about this project back in its earliest days—YOU ROCK.

To **every one** of the authors who risked their hearts to share their dog's story with the world—you are the heroes of *Gone Dogs*. Without you, this book wouldn't exist. Thank you.

To our families, who put up with us for so long as we took our lumps learning how to manage a project this big, HUGE props.

Thank you to Ken Wheaton, Judy Goldman, and Stephanie Whetstone, our volunteer judges who read every beautiful story and poem submitted. You're amazing. Really.

To Maya Myers, who helped ensure that 50 stories from 50 authors were all right and tight, thank you.

To Lee Clow for taking time to write our foreword—we can't thank you enough, sir.

And finally to you, our reader—thank you. We hope you find the stories as beautiful and inspiring as we do.

May you always have a dog by your side as you travel through life.

JIM and LAURIE

If you enjoyed Gone Dogs, *please consider leaving a review on Amazon or elsewhere to help others discover it. Thank you. Truly.*